T0329173

Cambridge Elements ≡

Elements in Corpus Linguistics
edited by
Susan Hunston
University of Birmingham

DOING LINGUISTICS WITH A CORPUS

Methodological Considerations for the Everyday User

Jesse Egbert
Northern Arizona University

Tove Larsson
Uppsala University / Northern Arizona University

Douglas Biber
Northern Arizona University

CAMBRIDGE
UNIVERSITY PRESS

CAMBRIDGE
UNIVERSITY PRESS

University Printing House, Cambridge CB2 8BS, United Kingdom

One Liberty Plaza, 20th Floor, New York, NY 10006, USA

477 Williamstown Road, Port Melbourne, VIC 3207, Australia

314–321, 3rd Floor, Plot 3, Splendor Forum, Jasola District Centre,
New Delhi – 110025, India

79 Anson Road, #06–04/06, Singapore 079906

Cambridge University Press is part of the University of Cambridge.

It furthers the University's mission by disseminating knowledge in the pursuit of
education, learning, and research at the highest international levels of excellence.

www.cambridge.org
Information on this title: www.cambridge.org/9781108744850
DOI: 10.1017/9781108888790

First published 2020

A catalogue record for this publication is available from the British Library.

ISBN 978-1-108-74485-0 Paperback
ISSN 2632-8097 (online)
ISSN 2632-8089 (print)

Doing Linguistics with a Corpus

Methodological Considerations for the Everyday User

Elements in Corpus Linguistics

DOI: 10.1017/9781108888790
First published online: October 2020

Jesse Egbert
Northern Arizona University

Tove Larsson
Uppsala University / Northern Arizona University

Douglas Biber
Northern Arizona University

Author for correspondence: Jesse Egbert, jesse.egbert@nau.edu

Abstract: Paradoxically, doing corpus linguistics is both easier and harder than it has ever been before. On the one hand, it is easier because we have access to more existing corpora, more corpus analysis software tools, and more statistical methods than ever before. On the other hand, reliance on these existing corpora and corpus linguistic methods can potentially create layers of distance between the researcher and the language in a corpus, making it a challenge to do linguistics with a corpus. The goal of this Element is to explore ways for us to improve how we approach linguistic research questions with quantitative corpus data. We introduce and illustrate the major steps in the research process, including how to: select and evaluate corpora; establish linguistically motivated research questions, observational units, and variables; select linguistically interpretable variables; understand and evaluate existing corpus software tools; adopt minimally sufficient statistical methods; and qualitatively interpret quantitative findings.

Keywords: corpus linguistics, research design, quantitative methods, qualitative methods, statistical methods

ISBNs: 9781108744850 (PB), 9781108888790 (OC)
ISSNs: 2632-8097 (online), 2632-8089 (print)

Contents

1 Introduction

The technological capabilities of corpora and corpus analysis methods have been increasing at an astounding rate, allowing practitioners to carry out research studies of a scope unimaginable just a few decades ago. One remarkable benefit of these resources is that the practicing researcher does not need technical expertise in computer science or engineering to perform corpus analyses. That is, corpora are now so readily available, and many corpus analysis tools are so user-friendly, that we are all able to carry out sophisticated corpus analyses with relative ease. In some respects, this state of affairs is similar to the practice of driving a car. That is, everyday drivers – with no expertise in engineering – can easily take advantage of advanced technologies relating to speed, reliability, and efficiency that have been engineered for modern automobiles.

However, although it requires no technical expertise in engineering to safely drive a car, it can often be useful to have some understanding of what goes on "under the hood". One reason for this is that – despite the best efforts of engineers – things go wrong, and it is nice to be able to fix simple problems yourself. For example, batteries die and tires go flat – and so it can be very useful to know how to jump-start a car or how to change a tire. A second reason is that it is possible for a driver to damage a car, and so it is nice to have an understanding of circumstances that might cause problems, such as driving with the emergency brake on or with low pressure in your tires. Thus, some understanding of how a car works can be a useful complement to the simple practice of getting behind the wheel and turning the key.

Practicing corpus linguists have also benefited from the technological resources and capabilities developed by experts over the last several years, including corpora, corpus analysis tools, and advanced statistical techniques for analysis of quantitative patterns. However, our argument in the present Element is that it is useful for all of us to have some idea of the basics. That is, the processes of driving a car from point A to point B and of using a computer to carry out a corpus analysis are alike in that they can be quite simple: turn the machine on, push a few buttons, and get the results. But we believe that the two processes are also similar in that things can go wrong; with a corpus analysis, a researcher can sometimes perform actions that cause problems. And, finally, the two processes are similar in that a basic understanding of the underlying principles and mechanisms can go a long way toward alleviating potential problems. That is, just understanding the nature and composition of the corpus used for analysis, the linguistic and quantitative characteristics of research questions, and the kinds of linguistic information provided by automatic tools can be of tremendous assistance when conducting and interpreting corpus analyses. These are the kinds of consideration that we take up in the present Element.

In addition, there is a further striking parallel between driving a car and carrying out corpus linguistic research: in many cases, the amazing technology is not capable of taking the user the whole way to their intended objective. For example, imagine that you wanted to climb Mt. Whitney (the highest mountain in the continental United States). You could fly to Los Angeles and rent a car to drive to the trailhead at Whitney Portal. Your car would be capable of driving the required 225 miles, climbing from sea level to 8,300 feet, in less than 4 hours – a remarkable accomplishment! But that is not your goal. To reach the summit, you would still have to hike an additional 11 miles and climb an additional 6,200 feet. Of course, if you did not have the technology of the modern automobile, it would have taken you many days (or weeks) just to get to the trailhead. But that does not mean that the technology provided all of the resources that you needed to achieve your goal.

Corpus linguistic research can be similar in this regard. Our ultimate research goals are linguistic in nature, for example learning in detail about a linguistic pattern. Corpus resources and analytical technology can usually take us most of the way toward achieving those goals. But, often, additional work is required to achieve the ultimate goal. In this Element, we discuss the parts of this enterprise that can be achieved by available technology as well as the parts that require additional work on the part of the researcher. In many cases, these involve the same considerations that we have already identified, such as an understanding of the actual composition of your corpus and of the nature of the quantitative findings automatically provided by corpus analysis tools.

These are the themes that we develop in the following sections: providing a basic understanding of considerations that underlie the resources and analytical methods of corpus linguistics, and discussing how everyday corpus researchers, with minimal advanced technical expertise, can take control of their research while also employing available resources. Along the way, we emphasize the importance of linguistics in our research enterprises. This will help us to avoid the "good enough" temptation; that is, the risk that we end up focusing on the quantitative results provided by the technological resources and forget to sufficiently consider the linguistics: What was the linguistic research question? Was our study designed to address that linguistic research question? Can we interpret the quantitative results as linguistic patterns? Can we illustrate those patterns from actual texts?

To address such considerations, the Element will be organized into the following brief sections. All content sections include one or more case studies that serve to illustrate and elaborate on key points; boxes containing "Key

Considerations" are provided at the end of each main section. In Section 2, we look at the corpus itself and steps that can be taken to ensure that the texts in the corpus actually represent the language varieties of interest. Section 3 focuses on the observational units and variables in corpus analysis and how these differ depending on the research question and the research design in a corpus study. In Section 4, we discuss the interrelationship between linguistically interpretable variables and the interpretability of our results. We also bring up the need for clear operational definitions of the constructs being investigated. Section 5 builds on this discussion to explore how there can be a disconnect between linguistically motivated research and the results provided by pre-existing corpus analysis tools. In particular, we highlight the need to design methods and analyses that address a motivated linguistic research question, rather than merely asking a question that can easily be answered by an available tool.

In Section 6, we tackle a more advanced topic: the ways in which sophisticated statistical analyses can sometimes create unnecessary distance between the quantitative analysis and the actual linguistic phenomena being described. We propose a minimally sufficient approach to statistical analysis with two characteristics: the researcher uses statistics that are no more nor less sophisticated than necessary to answer the research questions, and all results of statistical modeling are complemented by simple descriptive statistics that are directly interpretable in relation to the linguistic characteristics of particular texts. We develop this last point in greater detail in Section 7, stressing the importance of returning to the actual language in the texts of a corpus, to explain/interpret quantitative patterns and to illustrate all quantitative patterns from actual examples. Finally, Section 8 summarizes and synthesizes the major challenges and opportunities afforded by quantitative corpus linguistics.

Our intended audience for these discussions is all practicing corpus linguists. Many of these topics might, on first consideration, appear to be basic and thus appropriate only for novices. But we believe that a fuller understanding of basic principles would benefit most of us. After all, it is easy to drive thousands of miles without ever looking under the hood – and then discover that we don't know where to find the car jack when we need to change a tire. Similarly, it is easy to conduct numerous studies using available corpora and numbers from available software tools – and then discover that we don't really know what kinds of texts were in our corpus or, specifically, what linguistic characteristics were counted by the tool. These are considerations for both novice and seasoned practitioners. Thus, while the topics covered here might appear to be elementary, we hope that the considerations raised in the sections below will be of interest to all students and researchers in corpus linguistics.

2 Getting to Know Your Corpus

2.1 Introduction

What we learn about any given topic stems from the data we choose to analyze. The primary source of data in corpus linguistics is, of course, a corpus. Thus, as the corpus we choose (or build) will impact our results, it is imperative that we devote sufficient attention to this crucial step of the research design process. In this section, we will start by commenting on a topic that has received ample attention in corpus linguistics over the years, namely whether bigger is better when it comes to corpus size. After that, we will address a closely related but less commonly discussed topic: corpus composition and the importance of knowing what is in a corpus.

The size of a corpus has been a major focus for corpus creators and researchers since the earliest days of corpus linguistics. As most readers know, the first electronic corpus was the Brown corpus. The creators of the Brown corpus included a million words of written American English, which was a tremendous feat in the 1960s when it was created. At that point in time, there were no online repositories of digital texts, and computer memory and processing power was extremely limited. Since that time, there have been rapid advances in computing and text availability. It comes as no surprise, then, that we have seen a corresponding explosion in the creation and availability of increasingly large corpora. In the 1960s and 1970s, the largest electronic corpus in existence was the Brown corpus, containing 500 texts and a million words. Now we have much larger corpora; for example, the ENCOW corpus contains 16 billion words. Corpus size has been a major goal within corpus linguistics throughout its history. Much has been written on the topic of corpus size. In some cases, corpus scholars have advocated for a heavy focus on corpus size (Clear, 1992; Sinclair, 1991; Hanks, 2012). However, in other cases, the enthusiasm for very large corpora has been tempered by other considerations related to representativeness (see, e.g., Hunston, 2002; McEnery, Xiao, & Tono, 2006; Biber, 1993; Egbert, 2019).

It is clearly the case that, all other things being equal, a bigger corpus is preferable. If the balance of corpus composition is held constant, a larger corpus allows us to obtain higher, and thus more stable, frequency counts of linguistic features. And the larger corpus will likely include occurrences of additional word *types* and phrase *types* (i.e., new words and phrases not represented in the smaller corpus). However, in practice, we are rarely faced with a decision between two corpora with identical designs: a larger and a smaller one. That is, in reality, "all things" are almost never equal, and we have to make decisions based on the composition of the corpus.[1] The remainder of the present section examines ways in which we can approach such decisions and why they matter.

Our goal as corpus linguists is to carry out research on a corpus of texts that is as representative as possible of a target population of interest. Corpus linguists are interested in how language is actually used in a register, dialect, or entire language; therefore, it is not controversial that we want our corpus to be an accurate representation of that target register, dialect, or entire language. In other words, we use the corpus sample as a proxy for a language domain of interest, with the hope that we can glean from the corpus generalizable insights about language use in that domain. To do this, we can either (a) compile an appropriate corpus or (b) select an appropriate existing corpus.

In an ideal world, researchers would compile a new corpus for each research study they carry out. This is common in other disciplines, where study-specific samples allow the researcher to customize the design and the size of a sample to suit specific research question(s). However, the resources required to create a new corpus often make this an impractical choice in our field; as a result, it is common for researchers to reuse publicly available corpora across multiple studies. Thus, the major challenges facing many corpus researchers are selecting the most appropriate available corpus *and* recognizing its limitations vis-à-vis the research questions at hand.

The downside of reusing an available corpus is that no corpus is "one size fits all". A corpus contains a particular sample of texts, and it is important to keep this in mind as the composition of this text sample ultimately determines the linguistic population to which findings from the corpus can be generalized. For these reasons, it is crucial that we select a corpus that is appropriate – in terms of both composition and size – for our research questions. And, since no corpus will ever be a fully perfect match to the research questions and target population, it is also essential that we identify where mismatches may arise and then interpret the findings relative to the limitations of any mismatch.

Our choice of corpus should be based on the specific goals of the study and the alignment between the target discourse and the composition of the corpus sample. Ideally, we should never have to settle for a corpus that does not perfectly represent the target population of interest. However, we often have

---

[1] It is also important to note in this context that the size of a sample cannot remedy or compensate for sampling bias in the design of a corpus. Bias in a corpus exists when texts are being sampled from the wrong places or in the wrong quantities. Increasing the magnitude of a biased sample, without making any changes to that incorrect design, cannot make the sample a better representation of the population; it produces only a larger biased sample. In other words, increasing the size of a corpus sampled from the *wrong* language domain cannot get us closer to the *right* corpus sample; it can only get us more of the language we are *not* interested in. A biased sample will always be biased, no matter how large it is (see, e.g., Blair & Blair, 2015: 10–11).

to make compromises one way or another. In practice, those compromises can go in one of two ways: either (1) we are able to locate an available corpus that is similar to the target domain that we are interested in, and we are able to interpret our findings relative to the actual composition of that corpus (see Section 2.2 below), or (2) there is no available corpus that adequately represents our domain of interest, and thus we need to invest the extra time and effort required to build such a corpus. We will not cover corpus compilation in this section, but we refer interested readers to McEnery, Xiao, and Tono (2006, unit A8) for more information. Instead, our focus here is on the steps that we can all take to evaluate whether an available corpus is adequate for our research goals. In short, that process is based on determining the composition of the corpus, and evaluating the extent to which that composition matches our target domain of interest. It should be noted, though, that more than one corpus might meet the criteria if our target domain is broadly defined, and yet the composition of these corpora can be quite different. These differences can lead to different linguistic results, which means that we should make an informed decision when choosing among them.

Thus, we need to familiarize ourselves with the composition of a corpus before using it for research purposes. Although there are complicated linguistic/statistical methods that could be applied, there are also two steps that every end-user of a corpus should try to undertake for this purpose:

(1) Read and critically examine any metadata and documentation provided by the corpus compilers. This includes information about the texts themselves (e.g. register, text length, transcription conventions) and information about the language producers (e.g. age, gender, first-language background).
(2) Critically examine the actual texts included in the corpus.

Surprisingly, the steps can require more work than might be expected. The first step is sometimes difficult to carry out due to missing or insufficiently detailed documentation or metadata. But if the user is able to obtain a copy of the corpus, the second step should always be possible. In the case study below (Section 2.2), we illustrate the kinds of detective work required to accomplish these steps in order to demonstrate the importance of establishing this background information about a corpus.

2.2 Case Study: Determining the Textual Composition of Available Corpora

Our goal in this case study is to show how we can use corpus documentation, metadata, and texts to learn as much as possible about the composition of a corpus and its relationship to the target domain. This allows us to know what parts of the target domain are included in and excluded from the corpus. It also puts us in a position where we can more fully understand the linguistic findings that come from the corpus, as well as how to appropriately generalize those findings.

Let's imagine that we have the research goal of investigating the use of nominalizations[2] and linking adverbials[3] in the target domain of published academic writing. For many of us, the first step would be trying to find an existing corpus that represents this target domain. We can cast the net widely at first by making a list of corpora that are possible candidates for our target domain. We can then begin to narrow down our list by process of elimination. An inappropriate corpus can often be ruled out after no more than a cursory review. For example, based solely on its name, the British Academic Written English (BAWE)[4] corpus might appear to be a good candidate, but a closer look at the corpus description reveals that, while it fits within academic writing, it contains only unpublished writing by student writers.

Through an initial review of available corpora, we narrowed our list of candidates down to two available corpora: the academic sub-corpus of the British National Corpus 1994 (BNC_AC) and the academic sub-corpus of the Corpus of Contemporary American English (COCA_AC). Because our target domain of published academic writing is defined quite broadly, we could simply stop here by selecting either of these two corpora on the grounds that both corpora are exclusively composed of texts that are published, academic, and written. However, we believe it is crucial that researchers learn as much as possible about the corpus they plan to use. It is not enough to simply know that a corpus does not contain any texts that fall *outside* of the target domain. We also need to know the extent to which we have represented the full range of texts that exist *inside* of the target domain. Thus, we will probe deeper into these two corpora to explore what we can learn from their metadata, documentation, and texts.

---

[2] Nominalizations in this study are operationalized as derived nouns, or words that have become nouns through the addition of a derivational suffix. Specifically, we focus on a small subset of six possible derivational suffixes (see Table 2.2.). According to Biber, Johansson, Leech, Conrad, and Finegan (1999: 319): "Noun derivational suffixes, on the other hand, often do change the word class; that is, the suffix is often attached to a verb or adjective base to form a noun with a different meaning. There are, however, also many nouns which are derived by suffixes from other nouns".

[3] Linking adverbials are adverbials that function "to state the speaker/writer's perception of the relationship between two units of discourse. Because they explicitly signal the connections between passages of text, linking adverbials are important devices for creating textual cohesion" (Biber et al., 1999: 875). In this study, we include nine linking adverbials.

[4] www.coventry.ac.uk/research/research-directories/current-projects/2015/british-academic-written-english-corpus-bawe/

Information about BNC_AC can be found from several sources. There is documentation[5] published online for the BNC, as well as a Wikipedia page devoted to information about its design.[6] These sources tell us that there are many academic texts in the BNC. But it is hard to figure out what they actually are and what they represent. Fortunately, there is much more information in the headers of the corpus texts themselves, and the information has been summarized in spreadsheet format by Mark Davies on his site for the BNC.[7] If we click on the little paper icon at the top of the page and click the "Texts" link, we can review the spreadsheet, which is organized according to many different variables (e.g. genres, medium, domain). This information is very useful, and we encourage all corpus creators to document corpora in easily accessible ways such as this. We can also download the full BNC corpus[8] to review the actual texts.

The metadata for COCA_AC can all be acquired from a single site.[9] We can click on the little paper icon at the top of the page to get to summary information about the sub-corpora within COCA, including COCA_AC. For more detailed information about the individual texts, we can download a spreadsheet similar to the one for BNC_AC from the same site. For the academic component, this document gives us the name of the author, the title, source, and publication year of the text, along with information about the subgenres included. It would be very useful to review the content of the texts themselves; however, the online version of COCA does not allow us to do so.

Following the recommended steps outlined in the section introduction, we now use the information from the documentation and metadata for BNC_AC and COCA_AC to investigate the types of published academic writing they contain. To conserve space, we report these results together for the two corpora. However, the goal here is not for us to compare them. Remember that we have already established that both corpora are appropriate for our target domain of published academic writing.

Table 2.1 contains information about the composition of BNC_AC and COCA_AC according to subgenres, disciplines, and time periods, which are three examples of important variables to account for when examining a corpus of published academic writing. COCA_AC contains only journal articles. There are nearly 100 journals represented in the corpus. BNC_AC contains two different subgenres – books and journal articles – as well as a miscellaneous category. The books subgenre includes university textbooks as well as scholarly

[5] www.natcorp.ox.ac.uk/docs/URG/BNCdes.html#BNCcompo
[6] https://en.wikipedia.org/wiki/British_National_Corpus
[7] www.english-corpora.org/bnc/
[8] https://ota.bodleian.ox.ac.uk/repository/xmlui/handle/20.500.12024/2554
[9] www.english-corpora.org/coca/

Table 2.1 Meta-data for texts in BNC_AC and COCA_AC across subgenres, disciplines, and time

	BNC_AC		COCA_AC	
	Category	**Texts (%)**	**Category**	**Texts (%)**
Subgenres	Books	337 (67)	Journals	26,137 (100)
	Journals	153 (30)		
	Miscellaneous	15 (3)		
Disciplines	Politics/law/ education	186 (37)	Science/ technology	4,578 (18)
	Social sciences	142 (28)	Geography/ social sci.	4,053 (16)
	Humanities/arts	87 (17)	Education	4,033 (15)
	Natural sciences	43 (9)	Medicine	3,288 (13)
	Medicine	24 (5)	Humanities	3,116 (12)
	Tech/ engineering	23 (5)	History	2,350 (9)
			Law/politics	1,887 (7)
			Philosophy/ religion	1,513 (6)
			Miscellaneous	1,176 (4)
			Business	143 (1)
Time	1960–1974	6 (1)	1990–1999	9,073 (35)
	1975–1984	37 (7)	2000–2009	9,638 (37)
	1985–1995	461 (92)	2010–2019	7,426 (28)

monographs. The journal articles are all published in peer-reviewed journals. It is important to note that there are only twenty-one journals represented in this set, and 82% of the texts come from just six journals. The miscellaneous category includes various other text types such as legal reports, grants, and dissertations.

In terms of disciplinary variation, the journal articles in COCA_AC were selected from across the US Library of Congress classification system. In total, there are nine major disciplines and a miscellaneous category. The articles are distributed relatively evenly across these disciplines. The discipline categories in BNC_AC are defined broadly into five categories. The texts are not evenly divided among these disciplines. Eighty-one percent of the texts in BNC_AC fall into one of the "soft" sciences, which includes social sciences, humanities, and politics/law/education.

Most of the texts in BNC_AC were collected between 1985 and 1995, with a small number coming from earlier decades. The texts in COCA_AC are divided relatively evenly across the three decades of the 1990s, 2000s, and 2010s.

The BNC_AC texts contain a wealth of metadata included in the headers for the text files. This metadata includes author information, title, publication information, as well as a short descriptive summary of the text. This information can be used to further examine the contents and characteristics of the texts. The COCA_AC files contain no additional metadata. Each COCA_AC text file begins with a text ID that links them to the information in the spreadsheet we reviewed earlier.

As mentioned, there are two important reasons for carrying out the kinds of corpus evaluations we have demonstrated here. First, it is important to evaluate a corpus to determine whether it falls within the scope of the target language domain for a particular study (i.e. published academic writing, in this case). The second reason is less obvious. We must also understand the composition of a corpus so that we can understand the extent to which it represents the full range of text types that exist in the population. As we saw just now, COCA_AC and BNC_AC both fall squarely within the target domain of published academic writing. However, it was not until we pushed further that we learned what parts of that broad domain these two corpora actually represent. BNC_AC covers a wide range of publication types and time periods but is more limited in its coverage of academic disciplines. It is also notable that the texts in BNC_AC are unevenly distributed across categories within these variables. In contrast, COCA_AC is limited to only one publication type: journal articles. It contains a wide range of disciplines, as well as three decades of time period coverage, and it is well balanced across the levels of these variables. These facts should be used to inform the interpretation of linguistic results that come from these corpora, as well as the larger population they are generalized to. For example, findings from BNC_AC can be generalized to several different genres of academic writing, whereas COCA_AC can only be generalized to journal articles. In contrast, findings from COCA_AC can be generalized to a wide range of disciplines, while findings from BNC_AC are generalizable to a narrower set of disciplines. Finally, an obvious difference between these two sub-corpora is the dialect of English that they are meant to represent, with BNC_AC generally containing British English and COCA_AC generally containing American English.

It is worth asking whether all of this work is worth the effort. A skeptical reader may be wondering whether it is necessary to carry out a careful analysis of the composition of a corpus beyond simply confirming that it is appropriate for the target domain. One way to answer this question is by carrying out some linguistic analyses in these two corpora to explore whether there are any differences that can be attributed to corpus composition. So we return to the original research questions regarding the frequencies of nominalizations and

Table 2.2 Normed frequencies (per million words) for nominalizations in BNC_AC and COCA_AC

Query	COCA_AC	BNC_AC
tion_nn	18,220	18,995
sion_nn	2,740	3,010
ence_nn	3,382	4,117
ance_nn	2,328	2,225
ism_nn	1,103	1,195
ment_nn	5,863	6,071
Total	**33,636**	**35,613**

Table 2.3 Normed frequencies (per million words) for linking adverbials in BNC_AC and COCA_AC

Query	COCA_AC	BNC_AC
however	890	1,220
thus	477	551
therefore	288	583
moreover	130	126
consequently	56	60
accordingly	34	62
furthermore	102	96
hence	70	131
nevertheless	74	155
Total	**2,121**	**2,984**

linking adverbials in published academic writing. Table 2.2 contains the results for the nominalizations, including the exact queries run as well as results measured in frequencies per million words. BNC_AC uses more nominalizations overall. While this difference is not large, it is quite systematic, with the BNC_AC having higher frequencies for five of the six morphological endings. Table 2.3 reveals a similar trend, with BNC_AC using more linking adverbials overall and more for eight of the nine individual adverbials.

It appears that these features, which are strongly associated with academic writing (Biber et al., 1999), are more frequent in BNC_AC than in COCA_AC. We can revisit our description of the content of these corpora for possible explanations. Whereas BNC_AC contains a wide array of academic publication types, COCA_AC contains only one: journal articles. If we take a closer look at the journal articles in COCA_AC, we find that in some cases these articles are not the reports of scientific research that we might expect. One example is an article published in *Academic Questions* that contains the transcript of a lecture titled "The Sidney Hook Memorial Award Address: On the Self-Suppression of Academic Freedom". The first three sentences are:

> I must begin by saying this: In preparation for this lecture, I read (or in some cases reread) a number of the writings of Sidney Hook. I read them solely to give me the right starting point for a lecture given in honor of Sidney Hook. But instead I found myself infused with a set of ideas that were relevant to a different setting, a different occasion.

While the journal *Academic Questions* may be peer reviewed, this particular paper certainly was not because it is the verbatim transcript of a previously recorded speech.

Another example from COCA_AC is an article titled "Shania Twain Shakes Up Country Music" published in the *Journal of Popular Culture*. This article reads like a news article, or even a feature article in a celebrity magazine. It contains many personal quotes and slang terms (e.g. "flipped people out," "rips it, tears it, and shreds it"), all couched inside a fast-paced narrative commentary on a current celebrity:

> Of course, what flipped people out was the possibility that Twain was not a country artist but a carpetbagger. Most reviews of the third album made this point one way or another and used Twain's success as an occasion to lament the future of Nashville. Some reviewers were merely unappreciative and edgy, like David Zimmerman, who commented, "Shania Twain pushed the country envelope with her last album. With Come On Over . . . she rips it, tears it, and shreds it". But Rick Mitchell was utterly savage. He started with the "good news," about the abundance of tracks on the album. Then there was the bad news: "[S]he still sings like Shania Twain, which—with apologies to anyone who can actually carry a tune—means not much better than you or I".

Interestingly, as far as we can tell, both of these articles were published in peer-reviewed journals. That does not mean, however, that all of the articles published in them are peer reviewed. Nor does it mean that the same standards of double-blind peer review apply across all journals. It seems that COCA_AC contains a wide range of journals and article types from those journals. It would be good for users to know these characteristics when using this corpus. In contrast, all of the articles in BNC_AC appear to be examples of peer-reviewed articles. However, there is a much narrower range of disciplines represented in BNC_AC. For example, many of the texts in BNC_AC come from the journal *Gut: Journal of Gastroenterology and Hepatology*. The vocabulary, and even the grammar, in this journal will be distinct in particular ways. As a case in point, the word *intestine* occurs 3.02 times per million words in BNC_AC, and only 0.33 times per million words in COCA_AC. The composition of the corpus will be important for corpus users to know, especially if their primary interests lie in researching one or more disciplines that are not well represented in BNC_AC.

It appears that one major difference between BNC_AC and COCA_AC is how the texts themselves are collected. In the BNC_AC, each text was first reviewed for its suitability for the corpus and then assigned an appropriate genre category, regardless of where or how it was published. Using this process, if the creators of the BNC_AC had encountered the two texts we used as examples, they probably would *not* have classified them as peer-reviewed journal articles. It appears that the process for selecting texts in COCA_AC was different. While the process of text collection for COCA_AC is not as transparent as that for BNC_AC, it appears that rather than selecting texts based on a review of individual articles, the focus was on choosing journals that were available and listed as peer reviewed. Once those journals were identified, our best guess is that all available articles were downloaded automatically and incorporated into the corpus. This may be one reason for the presence of speech transcripts and celebrity news. Or, it is possible that these were included deliberately on the grounds that they are representative of published academic writing. It is difficult to be certain because the methods used to compile COCA_AC are not described in detail.

Our goal here has not been to criticize either BNC_AC or COCA_AC. To the contrary, we believe that both corpora are representative of published academic writing. The key is to notice how different they are, both in their composition and in their linguistic characteristics. In short, a corpus *is what it is*, and *it contains what it contains*. Based on the linguistic results presented here, it is clear that the composition of a corpus has an impact on its linguistic characteristics. Despite the fact that BNC_AC and COCA_AC both contain exclusively published academic writing, they are very different in their composition. These compositional differences result in linguistic differences. Neither corpus is correct – or incorrect – in its design; the two corpora are simply different in their composition. Our point is that it is crucial for corpus users to understand the design and composition of an existing corpus, for the purposes of (1) determining whether a corpus aligns with a target domain and (2) evaluating the extent to which a corpus represents the full range of text types from that target domain. In cases where no existing corpus is appropriate for the research question of interest, we encourage researchers to devote the time and effort required to create an appropriate and representative corpus. We also encourage corpus creators to be more transparent in documenting their corpora. In the case of COCA_AC, we get ample detail about the sources for the texts, but we know little about the methods that were used to determine that those were appropriate for the corpus. In the case of BNC_AC, we get useful information about the description of why texts were included and how they were classified, but we found it very difficult to get information about the publications that the texts were taken from.

2.3 Conclusion

To end where we began, the ultimate goal of corpus linguistics is not to learn about a particular corpus but to learn about a larger target domain or population of actual language use. This requires that the sample of texts included in a corpus represents that domain or population. It can be tempting to adopt a "good enough" approach and select an existing, yet less than ideal, corpus in hopes that results based on it can provide information about a more desirable population that it was not actually sampled from. Unfortunately, this is not how it works. Language varies in extreme ways across text varieties (e.g. dialects, registers, L1 backgrounds, disciplines) and undergoes change over time. As we saw, even two corpora that share many characteristics (published academic writing) can differ in important ways, both compositionally and linguistically. These types of difference make it impossible to use language from one particular variety or time period to represent another. Thus, as researchers who care first about representing actual language use in the real world, we must be devoted to representing that language use of interest in our corpus samples.

We wish to point out that there is often a sizeable gap between the ideal of perfect representativeness and the practical limitations (of time, money, text availability, copyright permissions, etc.) that we inevitably face when designing or selecting corpus samples. The ideal of representativeness may be more or less easy to achieve depending on the subfield of corpus linguistics (historical vs. present-day data; other languages vs. English; spoken vs. written; young learners vs. university students). We thus advocate for a pragmatic approach that aims for the ideal of representativeness (see Leech, 2007), makes accurate claims about the population that the corpus sample was actually drawn from, and acknowledges (and documents and reports) the limitations of the sample.

Furthermore, size is in and of itself *not* a good criterion for deciding which corpus to use. This is not to say, though, that size is not important. Once it has been determined that the composition of a corpus is appropriate, size becomes quite important because it determines whether there are enough instances of the linguistic features of interest to offer stable estimates of how those features are used in the full population. A very small corpus, no matter how well its design matches the composition of the population, cannot provide stable estimates. The most important points we want to make here about corpus size are that (a) it becomes relevant only *after* it has been determined that the corpus composition is appropriate and that (b) it depends on the particular linguistic feature(s) of interest.

For researchers who are attempting to identify an existing corpus to use in their research, we hope that the methods introduced here, and exemplified in the case study, will aid in the process of evaluating the appropriateness of candidate corpora. As we have shown in the case study, a "close enough" approach is not adequate. However, researchers can evaluate corpus appropriateness for themselves by critically examining corpus metadata and documentation, as well as the actual texts in the corpus.

Key Considerations:

- Corpus findings can be generalized to a larger discourse domain only if the composition of the corpus adequately represents that discourse domain.
- After we have decided that the composition of a corpus is adequately representative, we can evaluate its size based on the linguistic features being investigated.
- It is important to read and critically examine the metadata, documentation, and text files of a corpus to evaluate its representativeness before deciding to use it.

3 Research Designs: Linguistically Meaningful Research Questions, Observational Units, Variables, and Dispersion

3.1 Introduction

The present section discusses several topics required to understand how quantitative corpus analyses relate to tangible linguistic descriptions. The discussion builds on two underlying major concepts: *research designs* and *research questions*. The *research design* is the way in which quantitative linguistic data is collected and organized. The *research questions* specify what we want to learn about language use by doing a corpus analysis. It turns out that these are two sides of the same coin: The research questions dictate the research design. And, conversely, once data has been collected according to a particular research design, it can only be used to answer certain types of linguistic research questions. Unfortunately, novice researchers often end up with a mismatch: collecting data according to one type of research design but then attempting to analyze that data to answer a different type of linguistic research question.

To better understand how this mismatch can occur, we need to begin with the two basic components of all research designs: *observational units* and *variables*. *Observational units* (or just *observations*) are the units of language on which measurements are taken. Simply put, the observations are the linguistic objects being described in a study (e.g., words, grammatical features, texts). And *variables* measure linguistic characteristics of those observations.

The trickiest problem with corpus linguistic research designs is that the observations can be either linguistic tokens (i.e. each occurrence of a target word or target grammatical construction) or texts. If the observations are linguistic tokens, the variables identify linguistic characteristics of the token or the context (e.g. Is the token a noun or a verb? Does the token refer to an animate or an inanimate object? What is the word that occurs immediately after the token?). In contrast, if the observations are texts, the variables measure how often different linguistic features occur in each text. These represent fundamentally different types of research design, which can be used to answer fundamentally different kinds of research question.

One major type of corpus linguistic research question aims to describe the factors predicting the use of structural variants for a linguistic feature. For questions of this type, each token of the linguistic feature is an observation, and aspects of the linguistic context are analyzed as variables. For example, a researcher might be interested in relative clause constructions and what linguistic factors motivate the choice between *which*-relative clauses and *that*-relative clauses (see, e.g., Hinrichs et al., 2015). In this case, relative clauses are the observational units, and each occurrence of a relative clause would be one observation. The variables would measure factors in the linguistic context that might favor the choice of *which* versus *that*, such as the syntactic role of the head noun, and the syntactic role of the gap. Table 3.1 provides an example of data in this type of study; each row in the table represents information about one relative clause.

We refer to this kind of a study as a "variationist" research design. In most cases, the variables in a variationist design are *not* quantitative. For example, the

Table 3.1 Example of the data in a variationist study of *which*-relative clauses
vs. *that*-relative clauses

Relative pronoun	Syntactic role of the head NP	Syntactic role of the gap
that	subject	subject
that	direct object	direct object
which	direct object	subject
that	direct object	subject

variable "Syntactic role of the gap" can have values like "subject," "direct object," and "adverbial" – categories, rather than numeric values. However, in the statistical analysis, it is possible to count the frequency of each category and to compare those frequencies (e.g. the frequency of relative clauses with a subject gap vs. an object gap).

A second major type of corpus research design – referred to here as a "descriptive linguistic"[10] design – aims to describe the linguistic characteristics of different kinds of text. There are two subtypes of descriptive linguistic research design: "whole-corpus" and "text-linguistic". The simpler of the two subtypes is the whole-corpus research design, where the researcher computes rates of occurrence for linguistic features in different corpora (where each corpus represents a register or linguistic variety). For example, it would be possible to compute the rates of occurrence for *which*-relative clauses and *that*-relative clauses in a conversation corpus compared to a newspaper corpus. In this case, the corpora are the observational units, and the major linguistic variables (rates of occurrence for each type of relative clause) are quantitative.[11] We will discuss the "text linguistic" research design further down.

Although both variationist and descriptive linguistic research designs are associated with quantitative findings, the numbers have fundamentally different linguistic interpretations: indicating the proportional preference for a linguistic pattern in a variationist design, and indicating the extent to which a linguistic feature will be encountered in discourse in a "whole-corpus" design. We discuss this interpretive distinction in detail in the case study in Section 3.2 (see also Biber & Jones, 2009).

Before moving on to the case study, though, we need to introduce an additional foundational concept: *dispersion*. In a corpus study, dispersion statistics measure the extent to which linguistic phenomena are uniformly distributed across texts. This is not merely a technical detail. Rather, the evaluation of dispersion is an essential consideration for any researcher trying to determine whether frequent linguistic features are actually typical of the linguistic variety represented in the corpus (e.g. a register or dialect).

It is easy to illustrate the importance of dispersion for the study of frequent words. For example, the whole-corpus study reported in Carroll et al. (1971)

---

[10] Although the term "descriptive linguistic" has been used synonymously with exploratory, atheoretical research goals, we use it here to refer to quantitative research designs with the more specific research goal of describing the linguistic characteristics of different kinds of discourse.

[11] Rates of occurrence are computed by dividing the number of tokens by the total size of the corpus, and then multiplying by whatever basis is chosen for norming. For example, if there were 222 relative clauses in a 700,000-word corpus, and we have decided to normalize per million words, the normed rate of occurrence per million words would be: (222 / 700,000) * 1,000,000 = 317.14 per million words.

found that the words *chord(s)* and *origin(s)* were both relatively common in academic writing: *chord(s)* occurred c. 100 times per million words, and *origin(s)* occurred c. 50 times per million words. However, although it was more frequent, the word *chord(s)* was dispersed very unevenly across the texts of the corpus, occurring frequently only in texts about music (and occasionally in texts about math), and not occurring at all in texts from other sub-disciplines. In contrast, the word *origin(s)* was dispersed across texts from nearly all sub-disciplines. Thus, from the perspective of dispersion, the word *origins* is more typical of academic writing than the word *chords*.

In order to measure the dispersion for a linguistic feature, the corpus must be divided into smaller parts. Two approaches have been used for this task: (1) treating each text in the corpus as an observational unit and (2) dividing the corpus into arbitrary, equal-sized parts (often 100 parts). We strongly recommend the text-based approach because it is based on naturally occurring texts that are linguistically interpretable. In contrast, although the approach based on equal-sized parts is as much work as the text-based approach,[12] it cannot be interpreted in terms of linguistic units of discourse that occur in the natural world (see Egbert, Burch, & Biber, 2020). The most likely explanation for the persistence of arbitrary equal-sized parts is that Juilland's D, the most commonly used dispersion index, cannot be computed for unequal-sized parts. There are, however, other alternatives (e.g. Gries's DP; D_A) that are superior to Juilland's D in this and other ways (see Biber, Reppen, Schnur & Ghanem, 2016; Egbert et al., 2020).

In order to describe both rate of occurrence and dispersion in a meaningful way, we need a second subtype of descriptive linguistic research design, which we refer to as a "text-linguistic" design. The research goals associated with this design are similar to those in the "whole-corpus" approach: to describe the linguistic characteristics of different kinds of text. However, in a "text-linguistic" design, each text is an observational unit. As a result, this research design makes it possible to compute both the average rate of occurrence across all texts from a corpus as well as a measure of dispersion *across texts*, indicating the extent to which the linguistic feature is uniformly distributed across texts. Thus, a whole-corpus design and a text-linguistic design are similar in that both can provide a rate of occurrence: overall measures of how common a feature is in the corpus. However, the two design types are fundamentally different in their treatment of dispersion: it is not possible to analyze dispersion in a whole-corpus design, while analysis of dispersion is a central characteristic of

---

[12] This, of course, assumes that the corpus is actually composed of texts that are available to the author, which is not always the case.

the text-linguistic design. The case study in Section 3.2 provides a specific example to contrast the kinds of linguistic description possible in variationist, whole-corpus, and text-linguistic research designs.

3.2 Case Study: What Can We Learn about English Genitives in Variationist, Whole-Corpus, and Text-Linguistic Research?

The use of the genitive construction in English has been the focus of many corpus linguistic studies. Traditionally, researchers have studied two forms of the genitive in English: the *'s*-genitive (*the business's owner*) and the *of*-genitive (*the owner of the business*). In both cases, the construction consists of a head noun (e.g. *owner*) and a modifying noun phrase (NP) (*the business*).

Studies of English genitive constructions can be carried out employing any of the three major research designs discussed in Section 3.1. However, the linguistic research goals of variationist studies are fundamentally different from those of descriptive linguistic studies, including both whole-corpus and text-linguistic designs. And, as a result, the quantitative results produced by these differing approaches require fundamentally different linguistic interpretations.

In variationist studies, each token of a genitive construction is analyzed to identify key aspects of the linguistic context. That is, the study is based on a sample of genitives that is extracted from a corpus. Thus, each occurrence of the genitive is an observation, and contextual characteristics like the animacy of the head noun and the animacy of the modifying noun are key variables. In addition, each token can be coded for its dialect and the historical period when it was produced. Table 3.2 illustrates the data analyzed in this type of study; each row in the table represents information about one genitive phrase.

Based on data of this type, it is possible to carry out statistical analyses to determine the contextual factors that favor the choice of the *'s*-genitive versus

Table 3.2 Example of the data in a variationist study of *'s*-genitives vs. *of*-genitives

Genitive variant	Head NP	Modifying NP	Animacy of head NP	Animacy of modifying NP	Dialect	Historical period
of	*policy*	*government*	no	no	BrE	1960
of	*price*	*gasoline*	no	no	AmE	1960
's	*car*	*my sister*	no	yes	AmE	1990
's	*best friend*	*my son*	yes	yes	AmE	1990

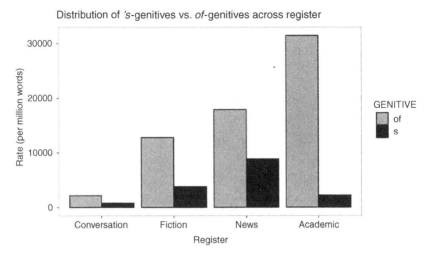

Figure 3.1 Rates of occurrence for *'s*-genitives and *of*-genitives in four registers

the *of*-genitive (see, e.g., Hinrichs & Szmrecsanyi, 2007; Szmrecsanyi & Hinrichs, 2008). For example, the presence of an animate (and especially human) modifying noun strongly favors the *'s*-genitive, while long modifying noun phrases favor the *of*-genitive.

In contrast, the whole-corpus approach directly analyzes the rate of occurrence for different linguistic features in different sub-corpora. In this case, each sub-corpus (e.g. a conversation corpus vs. an academic writing corpus) is an observation, and the normalized rate of occurrence for each construction type is a separate variable (i.e. the rates for *'s*-genitives and *of*-genitives). The research goal of this approach is to determine how often a linguistic feature occurs in the corpus overall, and how it varies according to variables such as register, dialect, or historical period. For example, Figure 3.1 displays the results of a whole-corpus analysis of four registers (adapted from Biber et al., 1999: 302 figure 4.6). Two major linguistic patterns emerge from these findings:

- *of*-genitives outnumber *'s*-genitives in all registers.
- Conversation has much lower rates of occurrence – for both *'s*-genitives and *of*-genitives – than any of the written registers (see Biber et al., 1999: 301).

As already noted, the research goals of variationist and whole-corpus studies are fundamentally different. And, in fact, their research designs permit answers to only certain kinds of linguistic research question. Variationist designs enable isolation of the contextual factors that favor a particular linguistic variant. But the quantitative results of a variationist study provide no information about the rates of occurrence in actual language use. In contrast, the quantitative results from whole-corpus designs directly tell us how commonly we will encounter a linguistic feature in discourse, but they offer no information relating to the contextual factors favoring one linguistic feature over another.

Unfortunately, because both types of study produce quantitative findings, it can be extremely easy to become confused about the linguistic generalizations that are appropriate for each research design. This is especially the case for variationist studies that compare linguistic patterns across sub-corpora.

As a result, the claimed conclusions about genitive constructions in some variationist studies appear to directly contradict the conclusions of whole-corpus studies. For example, in contrast to the patterns observed in Figure 3.1, variationist studies have concluded that the *s*-genitive is "frequent," especially in spoken English, especially in AmE, and especially in recent historical periods [**emphasis added**]: "The *s*-genitive is, on the whole, **more frequent** in spoken data than in written' (Szmrecsanyi & Hinrichs, 2008: 297); "Two further characteristics of our AmE material . . . are nonetheless likely to also be responsible for the **high frequency** of the *s*-genitive especially in Frown" (Hinrichs & Szmrecsanyi, 2007: 468); "[B]y 1991, the *s*-genitive had overtaken the *of*-genitive **in frequency** in both AmE and BrE" (Leech, Hundt, Mair, & Smith, 2009: 225). In part, the source of this confusion can be traced back to the word "frequency". If a linguistic feature is "frequent," we can expect that we will encounter that feature often in texts. This is the linguistic interpretation of "whole-corpus" quantitative findings. In contrast, though, "frequent" in variationist studies should be interpreted to mean that one variant is used a high proportion of the time relative to the other variant. The following quote makes this linguistic interpretation explicit: "We can observe that since the 1960s, the **relative frequency** of the *s*-genitive has increased substantially in both BrE (37 percent to 46 percent) and – even more markedly – in AmE (36 percent to 53 percent)" (Hinrichs & Szmrecsanyi, 2007: 448). The primary problem here is that a high proportion (or high relative frequency) does not necessarily correspond to a high rate of occurrence in texts. For example, Figure 3.2 is based on the same data as Figure 3.1, but it presents proportional use rather than rate of occurrence. From Figure 3.2, we might conclude that the *s*-genitive has a higher relative frequency in conversation than in academic writing, because it accounts for a higher proportion of all genitives. However, because genitive constructions are overall so rare in conversation, the actual rate of occurrence for *s*-genitives in conversation is much lower than in academic writing (see Figure 3.1).

As we noted in Section 3.1, there are actually two different research designs that can be used to describe the rates of occurrence of linguistic features in discourse. The whole-corpus design, illustrated in the present case study, is the simplest approach, treating each sub-corpus as an observation. The primary

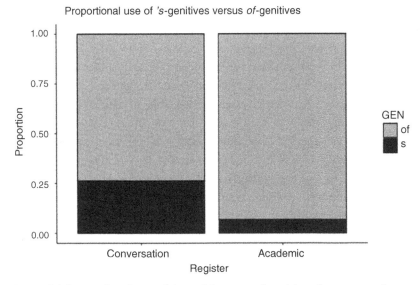

Figure 3.2 Proportional use of *'s*-genitives vs. *of*-genitives in conversation vs. academic writing

advantage of this approach is that it is very efficient because available concordancing tools can easily compute whole-corpus rates of occurrence. However, there are disadvantages of this approach. One major disadvantage is that it is not possible to compute a statistical measure of dispersion, making it difficult to determine the extent to which the use of a feature varies across texts within a sub-corpus.

The text-linguistic design can answer the same linguistic research questions, but additionally it can tell us whether a feature is uniformly distributed across the texts of a corpus. In the text-linguistic design, each text is an observation. Rates of occurrence for each linguistic feature are then computed for each text. Subsequently, it is possible to compute the average rate of occurrence for a register, as well as a measure of dispersion showing how much variation there is among the texts within a register. For example, Figure 3.3 displays boxplots for the use of *of*-genitives in science articles, providing information about the central tendency as well as the range of variation in each century. The box displays the interquartile range, the mean is marked by the plus sign, and the median is marked by the horizontal black line inside the box; the white dots represent outliers. In addition to concluding that the overall rate of occurrence for *of*-genitives decreased from the nineteenth to the twentieth century, these findings from a text-linguistic design would also permit us to conclude that the norms of use are becoming more established, reflected by a smaller range of variation among texts in the twentieth century than in the 18th and 19th centuries.

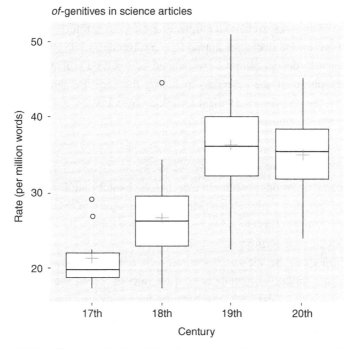

Figure 3.3 Distribution of *of*-genitives in science articles across centuries in the ARCHER corpus.

In past practice, the text-linguistic design has been rarely employed by corpus linguists, despite its apparent descriptive advantages. This limitation can be attributed to the heavy reliance on available concordancing tools by most corpus researchers. While it is relatively easy to obtain whole-corpus rates of occurrence using these tools, it is much more difficult to compute separate rates of occurrence for each text in a corpus. As a result, many corpus linguists tend to disregard the existence of texts in a corpus, instead treating the corpus itself as the primary object of study. We return to this theme repeatedly in the following sections.

3.3 Conclusion

In this section, we have introduced important concepts in research design, including research questions, observational units, and variables. We have distinguished between variationist and descriptive linguistic research studies, and shown how the two require different research designs that answer different research questions and offer different, albeit complementary, perspectives on language data. We made a further distinction within descriptive linguistic research studies between whole-corpus and text-linguistic research designs, and showed that while the whole-corpus approach is efficient and convenient, it is limited in the information it can provide about dispersion across texts in a corpus. We urge researchers in corpus linguistics to carefully consider these important issues and decisions during the research design phase. The importance of research design cannot be overstated as it plays a crucial role in every subsequent phase of the research, including the measurement of variables (Section 5), the choice of statistical techniques (Section 6), and the interpretation of linguistic findings (Section 7).

Key Considerations:
- Research questions should drive decisions about the choice of observational unit, how variables are defined, and the choice of research design.
- Observational units can be defined at the level of the linguistic feature, the text, or the corpus.
- Variables can be measured qualitatively, according to variants of a linguistic feature, or quantitatively, using rates of occurrence for features.
- Results from a variationist research design have a dramatically different interpretation from those from descriptive linguistic research designs.
- The text-linguistic research design has many advantages over the whole-corpus research design, including the possibility of measuring dispersion across meaningful corpus parts.

4 Linguistically Interpretable Variables

4.1 Introduction

In the present section, we discuss the need to ensure that all variables used in a corpus study are linguistically interpretable. A linguistic variable is interpretable when its scale and values represent a real-world language phenomenon that can be understood and explained. There are several specific challenges related to this goal. First is the need to ensure that all variables have clear operational definitions, including discussion of any mismatch between the constructs being investigated and the phenomena that are actually measured.[13] For example, if the extralinguistic variable of "register" included the values of "conversation" and "academic writing," we would need operational definitions for those

---

[13] However, while not addressed in this Element, measurement error is unavoidable even with clearly defined variables. Manually coding for variables is an oft-employed method in corpus linguistics that leads to measurement error. Increased transparency about decisions made during this process, including tests for intra- and inter-rater reliability, is highly recommended (see Larsson, Paquot, & Plonsky, forthcoming, for a more detailed discussion).

varieties. These definitions are closely related to the issues of corpus representativeness discussed in Section 2.

As we shall see, it is not enough to provide operational definitions just for the *extralinguistic* variables in a study; we also require precise operational definitions for the *linguistic* variables. For categorical variables, variationist studies of genitives like Hinrichs and Szmrecsanyi (2007) and Szmrecsanyi and Hinrichs (2008) are exemplary models of how each variable should be fully documented to specify exactly what phenomena are included/excluded from the analysis. For example, in the 2008 study, the linguistic variable *animacy* was operationally defined with four levels, which were evaluated to ensure that raters could distinguish among the categories with high reliability (p. 298).

Linguistic variables in descriptive linguistic research designs also require operational definitions. For example, it might seem that a grammatical construct like "relative clause" requires no operational definition. However, without discussion, the reader would not know whether the variable includes only finite relative clauses (e.g. *the construction that was analyzed in the 2007 study*) or both finite and non-finite relative clauses (e.g. *the finding discussed in the 2008 study; the person to see*). It turns out that nearly every linguistic feature requires an operational definition before it can be analyzed in a text-linguistic study (see fuller discussion in Biber & Conrad, 2019: 60–2).

The issues discussed so far in this section relate to the research methods required to ensure that quantitative variables are fully interpretable in linguistic terms. However, as will be discussed in more detail in Section 5, this interpretability becomes even more important when a researcher relies on measures that are automatically computed by corpus analysis software.

To illustrate the points made in this section introduction, we present two short case studies in Sections 4.2 and 4.3. In the first, we discuss corpus-based analyses of collocation, which often rely on complex statistical measures that can be difficult to interpret in linguistic terms. The second case study discusses measures of "keyness," which can present different types of challenges for meaningful linguistic interpretation.

4.2 Case Study 1: Measures of Collocation

The question that we explore in this case study is what quantitative measure is best suited to a particular research goal, using a major application of corpus research, namely the study of "collocation": "a relationship of habitual co-occurrence between words" (Stubbs, 1995: 1). One primary goal of such research has been to study the extended meanings of words beyond traditional dictionary definitions. For example, the verb *cause* is traditionally defined in neutral terms as "make something happen". However, corpus research shows that this verb frequently co-occurs with words referring to negative events, such as *trouble* or *problems*, a pattern first observed by Stubbs (1995) (see also, e.g., Hunston, 2007; Xiao & McEnery, 2006). These "collocates" of the word *cause* lead to the extended meaning of *cause*: "make something bad happen".

In many cases, it can be difficult to study the collocates of a target word by simply identifying the most frequent co-occurring words because those words might also simply be frequent in absolute terms, and therefore they are not very informative regarding the extended meaning of the target word. For example, a search in COCA on the most frequent words that occur immediately following the lemma *cause* results in the following list of function words: *of, by, the, a, for, and, it, you, to, that, him*. These function words will be frequent following almost any noun or verb in English, and thus they tell us little about the specific meanings of the word *cause*.

For these reasons, most research on collocation relies on statistical association measures instead of simple frequency. In short, these measures have been developed to identify "true" collocations: words that are actually attracted to one another rather than words that just happen to co-occur. As described by Evert (2004, 2009), there are over twenty different statistical measures that have been developed to identify the "true" collocates of a target word (including MI score, *t*-score, log-likelihood ratio, odds ratio, and Dice coefficient). For the most part, these measures all share the property that they compare the frequency of two words when they co-occur versus the frequencies of each word occurring by itself.[14] If the frequency of the co-occurring pair is higher than expected by chance (i.e. tokens of the co-occurring pair make up a high proportion of the individually occurring words), then the combination will have a large association score. For this reason, strongly associated words are often not frequent in absolute terms.

For example, the words with highest associations to the word *cause* in COCA_AC (based on MI scores) include *botulism, bloating, strep, diarrhea*. *Botulism* occurs only 214 times in the entire corpus, and 16 of those occurrences follow the word *cause*. Thus, although the co-occurring sequence *cause* botulism* (the lemma *cause* followed by *botulism*) does not occur often, it does reflect a strong collocational association because the pair co-occurs much more often than would be predicted by random chance.

It is difficult to choose the "best" measure of collocational association, even for expert statisticians (see discussion in Evert, 2004, 2009). One major

---

[14] In addition, the formulas for most measures include some type of logarithmic transformation, to adjust for the effect of extremely rare combinations.

challenge in making that choice is trying to understand the differing linguistic interpretations of each different association measure, and using that information to decide which measure is best suited to a particular research goal.

The question that we explore in this case study is what quantitative measure – an association measure or a frequency approach – is best suited to a particular research goal. It is worth noting that some researchers adopt a hybrid approach in which an association measure is used in conjunction with a minimum frequency. However, this is often not the case, and many studies rely on only association measures or frequency. As will be shown, the two kinds of measure tell us different things: The association measure tells us what words co-occur with the target word more often than we would expect by chance, even though the combination will usually not be frequent in absolute terms. In contrast, the simple frequency measure tells us how the target word is usually characterized in discourse, even though the two words might not be unusually "associated". Both of these goals might be useful for a discourse analysis, but their linguistic interpretations are fundamentally different.

To illustrate, we explored the way that *man* and *woman* are characterized in COCA_AC based on the words that precede each target word.[15] The first approach was to identify the words that occurred most frequently in the preceding position, excluding function words. As Table 4.1 shows, many of these words were commonly used to characterize both *man* and *woman*, including words like *young*, *old*, *black*, and *white*. These combinations are all very frequent in the corpus. For example, *young man* occurs c. 17,000 times and *young woman* occurs c. 10,000 times. In addition, the frequency approach identifies some words that were especially common with only one of these two target words (e.g. *dead man* and *beautiful woman*).

The results of this frequency approach can be contrasted with the results of an association measure approach (employing MI scores),[16] also shown in Table 4.1. One of these words – *unidentified* – was included on the lists for both the frequency and the MI approach, characterizing both *man* and *woman*. Otherwise, there are no similarities between the results of the frequency approach and those of the MI approach. The associated words identified by the MI approach are all relatively rare, sometimes occurring as infrequently as ten times in the corpus. It further turns out that some of these words occurred in

---

[15] For a more extended analysis of the collocates of *man* and *woman*, see Caldas-Coulthard & Moon (2010).

[16] Previous research has shown that the MI score disfavors high-frequency words (Biber, 2009). Hence, other alternatives have been proposed, including *t*-scores and log-likelihood. We chose to use MI scores here because they are still widely used in corpus linguistics, and they are the default measure of association strength in prominent tools, including the English-Corpora.org online interface.

Table 4.1 High-frequency words preceding *man* and *woman* in COCA_AC, respectively, as identified by a frequency vs. an association measure approach

Preceding word	Top 10 most frequent with *man*	Top 10 most frequent with *woman*	Top 10 MI scores with *man*	Top 10 MI scores with *woman*
young	***	***		
old	***	***		
unidentified	***	***	***	***
black	***	***		
white	***	***		
older	***	***		
good	***			
big	***			
dead	***			
little	***			
beautiful		***		
pregnant		***		
American		***		
elderly		***		
penisless			***	
red-robed			***	
window-shade			***	
grown-ass			***	
three-armed			***	
Vitruvian			***	
Kennewick			***	
repo			***	
distinguished-looking			***	
middle-aged				***
Canaanite				***
auburn-haired				***
gray-haired				***
short-haired				***
145-pound				***
pleasant-looking				***
fortyish				***
full-figured				***

only a single text (e.g. *penisless man* and *window-shade man*). The set of words most strongly associated with *man* is quite distinct from the set of words most strongly associated with *woman*. But given their rarity as well as their restricted distribution across texts, it would be hard to argue that these words are representative of the ways in which men and women are typically characterized in discourse. One potential method for dealing with this would be the hybrid approach just described, which relies on both a minimum frequency threshold and the analysis of association statistics.

In summary, the simple frequency approach to collocation is arguably more appropriate for the purpose of discourse characterization than statistical collocational measures. Regardless, the two certainly produce different results and require different linguistic interpretations. Our main goal in this case study is not to argue for one or the other approach. Rather, we hope to emphasize two general points: (1) the importance of understanding the linguistic interpretation of quantitative measures and (2) the importance of choosing the measure that best serves the purposes of your linguistic research question. We expand on this analysis of *man* and *woman* in Section 7.

4.3 Case Study 2: The Linguistic Interpretation of "Keyness" Measures

This second case study has a somewhat different focus from the previous one. In the previous study, we concentrated on the linguistic interpretation of different quantitative ways of capturing the same linguistic phenomena: the association between two words. In the present case study, by contrast, we turn to a method that can lead to different types of challenge for meaningful linguistic interpretation: "keyword analysis". This type of analysis is one of the most commonly used methods in corpus-assisted discourse analysis (see Egbert & Biber, 2019). The primary goal of keyword analysis is to identify a set of words that is especially characteristic of a type of discourse, or that provides insights into the "aboutness" of that discourse domain.

There are many different measures that have been used to identify keywords (see Gabrielatos, 2018), and the linguistic basis of those measures is often not easily interpretable. The standard practice is to measure "corpus frequency keyness", identifying words that are statistically more frequent in a target corpus than in a reference corpus.[17] Similar to collocational measures, a word could be identified as "key" even though it is not frequent in absolute terms or

---

[17] It should be noted that Scott's (1997) method of key-keyword analysis was an early attempt at incorporating dispersion into a corpus frequency keyness method. See Egbert and Biber (2019) for more discussion of this and other methods.

well-dispersed across texts. Rather, the primary consideration in the corpus frequency keyness approach is that the word needs to be statistically more frequent in the target corpus than in the reference corpus – a requirement that can be difficult to interpret linguistically.

The primary focus of the present case study is on the role of texts in keyword analysis. A second way in which traditional keyword analyses are similar to collocational analyses is that they usually treat the entire corpus as the unit of observation, giving no attention to the question of whether words are dispersed across the texts of a corpus.[18] As a result, the list of keywords produced in a corpus frequency keyword analysis does not necessarily represent the patterns found in most texts. That is, a word can be awarded a high keyness value if it occurs with a high frequency in a single text. Words such as these do not represent general discourse patterns across texts from a discourse domain.

An alternative approach for keyword analysis – text dispersion keyness – was introduced by Egbert and Biber (2019). Relative to the research goals described in Section 3 of this Element, text dispersion keyness has two major advantages: (1) it takes into account the dispersion of a word across the texts of a corpus and (2) it is therefore more directly interpretable in linguistic terms than traditional measures. This interpretability stems from the fact that a text is a valid unit of language production, but a corpus is not.

The specific methods used to compute text dispersion keyness are presented in Egbert and Biber (2019: 84–7). In brief, text dispersion keyness disregards corpus frequency entirely and focuses instead on identifying words that are used in significantly more texts in the target corpus than in the reference corpus. By focusing on the range of texts within the corpus that contain a given word, rather than the number of occurrences of that word in the corpus as a whole, Egbert and Biber hypothesized that the approach would identify words that typify the texts in a given domain, rather than words that occur frequently but do not actually typify the domain. This hypothesis was tested on a keyword analysis of a corpus of travel blogs, compared to a general reference corpus of web documents. Keywords were identified using four different traditional measures based on frequency, and those results were then compared with the keyword list produced by the text dispersion keyness approach. Egbert and Biber used quantitative and qualitative methods to compare the lists produced by

---

[18] However, despite this standard methodological approach, most discourse analysts are likely to agree that the text should be the primary focus of Corpus Assisted Discourse Studies (CADS). As a result, scholars like Baker (2004, 2010) insist on a text-dispersion requirement to complement keyness measures when carrying out a keyword analysis.

the traditional corpus frequency keyness method with those from the new text dispersion keyness method in terms of their:

1. relative frequency
2. relative dispersion
3. content-distinctiveness
4. content-generalizability.

In general, the top 100 keywords identified by the text dispersion method were both less frequent and less widely dispersed than the top 100 keywords identified through the traditional approaches. While this finding was surprising at first, the important considerations here are the *relative* frequency and the *relative* dispersion. Many of the keywords identified by the traditional frequency-based methods were common words that were frequent and dispersed widely in both the travel-blogs target corpus and the reference corpus. This is an interesting finding because we expected the frequency-based keywords to be poorly dispersed – and indeed many of them were poorly dispersed (see later in this section) – but we did not expect this method to produce many keywords that were frequent *and* well-dispersed. Importantly, these words were frequent and well-dispersed in both the target and the reference corpora. In contrast, the text dispersion keywords tended to be much more widely dispersed, as well as more frequent, in the travel-blog corpus than in the reference corpus. Thus, although the absolute frequencies and the dispersion rates of the text dispersion keywords tended to be lower than the words identified with frequency methods, the relative frequencies and the relative dispersion rates were much higher.

The equally convincing test of the text dispersion approach was its linguistic interpretability – the extent to which the method actually achieved the goal of capturing the "aboutness" of the target discourse domain. This was evaluated through comparisons of the content-distinctiveness and the content-generalizability of the keyword lists; the results showed that the text dispersion method was much better suited to the linguistic research goals. For example, the frequency-based approaches all identified multiple function words and multiple high-frequency verbs (e.g. *be, have, do, make, take, say, go*) in their keyword lists – words that are not especially distinctive for any particular discourse domain. Those methods similarly identified abbreviations and proper nouns in their lists – words that are likely to be peculiar to a specific text rather than generalizable across an entire discourse domain. In contrast, the text dispersion method identified only one function word and no high-frequency verbs, abbreviations, or proper nouns.

More qualitative analyses also supported the improved content-distinctiveness and content-generalizability of the text dispersion keyword lists. For example, a large majority of the words identified with this approach were clearly associated with the topical domain of travel blogs, including words that refer to modes of transportation (e.g. *bus*, *walk*, *boat*, and *flight*), geographical features (e.g. *beach*, *island*, *river*, *mountain*, and *sea*), activities and attractions for tourists (e.g. *park*, *museum*, *hiking*, *attractions*, *restaurants*, *swimming*, and *exploring*), language for describing travel locations (e.g. *amazing*, *beautiful*, *scenic*, *stunning*, *sunny*, and *spectacular*), and words related to food and dining (e.g. *beer*, *delicious*, *dinner*, and *lunch*). In contrast, the frequency methods identified numerous words that were either not distinctive for the target discourse domain (e.g. *a*, *along*, *back*, *be*, *had*, *his*, *not*, *we*, *will*) or clearly not generalizable to the entire domain (e.g. *Contiki*, *Krakow*, *Madrid*, *Paphos*, *Thailand*).

Traditional keyness measures are designed with the linguistic goal of identifying words that are especially reflective of the topics discussed in a discourse domain. It is reasonable to expect that words that are frequent in a domain would reflect the topics of that domain. However, that expectation is based on analysis of the entire corpus as a single unit of observation, disregarding the existence of texts in the corpus. Basing analyses on simple corpus frequency runs the serious risk of identifying patterns that are extremely common in a few texts but not generalizable across an entire discourse domain. In contrast, the text-linguistic approach – analyzing the linguistic characteristics of each text and then generalizing across texts – is much more representative of the linguistic patterns that exist across a discourse domain.

4.4 Conclusion

The present section emphasized the need for linguistically interpretable variables in all corpus linguistic studies. Specifically, we need to ensure that all variables – linguistic and extralinguistic alike – have clear operational definitions, with studies discussing any mismatch between the linguistic constructs of interest and what is actually being measured. The section also showed how our choice of approach should be aligned with our specific research goal(s).

Key Considerations:
- All linguistic variables need to have clear operational definitions.
- We should include discussion of any mismatches that exist between the constructs being investigated and the variables that are actually measured.
- Our methods for measuring variables should always be aligned with our research goal(s).

5 Software Tools and Linguistic Interpretability

5.1 Introduction

The large amounts of data typical of most empirical corpus linguistics studies necessitate computational tools to help process them. To this end, we can either use existing software tools or, assuming we have the skills required, develop our own programs. In general, the field tends to rely heavily on pre-existing software tools. These tools thus have a strong influence on current research practices in quantitative corpus linguistics, which means that it is of the utmost importance that we critically examine the results they provide.[19] In this section, we approach the topic from two angles – accuracy and transparency – to illustrate why it is important to be aware of what is going on "under the hood" when we use the tools to draw linguistic conclusions. Specifically, we discuss some pitfalls associated with commonly used software tools and suggest ways for the field to move forward.

A point of general knowledge is that it is difficult, if not impossible, for any tool to achieve perfect accuracy (measured through precision and recall),[20] meaning that we should make sure to test (and report) the precision and recall and not just accept results at face value. This becomes even more important when tools are applied to data that they were not developed for. For example, most taggers and parsers are developed for and trained on native-speaker Standard English data, which means that other varieties of English and learner writing may cause great difficulties for these tools, thus compromising their accuracy. As a case in point, Picoral et al. (forthcoming) compared the performance on second-language (L2) data of three tools used for linguistic annotation: the Stanford Dependency Parser (Chen & Manning, 2014), the Biber Tagger (e.g. Biber, 1988, 2006), and the Malt Parser (Nivre et al., 2007). For noun-noun sequences (e.g. *university students*), the Stanford Parser exhibited 92 percent precision, compared to 91 percent for the Malt Parser and 80 percent for the Biber Tagger, whereas the Biber Tagger exhibited 83 percent recall, compared to 67 percent for the Stanford Parser and 60 percent for the Malt Parser. Thus, if we had used the output of any of these parsers to draw conclusions about noun-noun

---

[19] However, it is of course important to keep in mind that even very reliable tools are only as good as the corpus used (see Anthony, 2013, for a discussion of corpus vs. tools). If we start out with a corpus that is not appropriate for the research question we pose, no tool – existing or new – will be able to remedy that (see Section 2).

[20] Precision measures "exactness" in that high precision means that the tool identified a high proportion of relevant results (e.g. when the word *mark* is coded as a noun, how often is it in fact a noun rather than a verb?); recall measures "relevance", and high recall means that a large fraction of the total number of relevant results were found (i.e. how often is the word *mark* used as a noun in cases that the automatic tagging failed to identify?). Precision and recall can vary independently.

sequences in L2 data, these conclusions would not have provided a particularly clear picture of what is actually in the data. And what is worse, if we had not tested the tools for precision and recall, we would not even have known that there are problems with the conclusions drawn.

A less frequently acknowledged fact is that classification errors are not likely to be distributed randomly across all features. If a grammatical tagger has an overall reported accuracy rate, it does not necessarily follow that *all* words and *all* features of the tag set are coded with that level of accuracy. For example, it might be the case that a tagger manual reports an accuracy rate of 94 percent for lexical verbs. But if you are interested specifically in lexical vs. auxiliary uses of the verb *do*, a tagger may actually perform significantly worse for this particular word/feature. The accuracy level may also vary across dialects and registers. We therefore recommend that researchers always carry out tests of accuracy, measured and reported in terms of both precision (relevant hits out of retrieved hits) and recall (retrieved hits out of the total number of relevant instances), specific to the linguistic feature(s) and varieties of interest.

However, while accuracy certainly is a threat to the validity of our results, perhaps the most serious risk to researchers using available tools is that many of the quantitative measures provided by corpus analysis software do not have transparent linguistic interpretations. In some cases, these are measures that have no direct counterparts in linguistic theory; in other cases, these are omnibus measures that collapse the use of multiple linguistic constructs into a single quantitative value. For example, many quantitative measures computed automatically by Natural Language Processing (NLP) software tools like Coh-Metrix (Graesser, McNamara, & Louwerse, 2003) and the L2 Syntactic Complexity Analyzer (L2SCA; Lu, 2010, 2017) are very difficult to interpret in a linguistically meaningful way, even if they may be presented by researchers using them as if they had straightforward linguistic interpretations. This will be exemplified in the case study in Section 5.2. Nonetheless, it is always the responsibility of the researcher – not the tool developer or anyone else – to ensure the accuracy of interpretations.

5.2 Case Study: Problems with Opaque Measures

In this case study, we illustrate some of the potential problems of relying on measures that are automatically calculated by corpus analysis software. The case study provides a "behind-the-scenes view" of the initial analysis of data from a recent study (Larsson & Kaatari, 2020), to illustrate why it is risky to simply accept the interpretations of automatic measures provided by corpus tools.

Larsson and Kaatari (2020) investigates a topic that has received extensive attention in the field of second language acquisition, namely *grammatical complexity*, here defined as "the addition of structural elements to 'simple' phrases and clauses" (Biber, Staples, Gray, & Egbert, 2020). In the study, L2SCA (Lu, 2010, 2017) was used as a first step to explore how the measures were patterned across registers and how they were used in learner writing. However, it quickly became apparent that the program could not provide sufficient information for a detailed linguistic analysis of the results.

As the output that was provided for each text did not provide sufficient information for the aims of Larsson and Kaatari's study, the authors went on to use the online mode of the program, which allows for sentence-by-sentence tagging, in order to try to isolate the different measures and thus decode the numeric scores provided by L2SCA. However, even with this approach, several questions remained unanswered, in part because interpreting the measures themselves proved more of a challenge than anticipated. One of the most important predictor measures for the goals of Larsson and Kaatari's study, *complex nominals per T-unit*, will be used here to illustrate this point.

Complex nominals per T-unit is a ratio-based measure. The challenges associated with ratio-based measures are discussed further down. However, even in isolation, the numerator (*complex nominals*) and the denominator (*T-units*) pose problems for the linguistic interpretability of the results.

Complex nominals is described as a measure that covers structures including nouns plus adjectives, possessives, prepositional phrases, relative clauses, participles, or appositives; it also includes nominal clauses (complement clauses controlled by verbs), and gerunds and infinitives when found in subject position (Lu, 2010: 483). In addition to confounding a large number of structurally and syntactically distinct grammatical features (see Biber et al., 2020), the exploratory analysis indicated that the measure was dichotomous, meaning that a noun phrase was coded as a "complex nominal" if it had any of the above characteristics. As a result, the sentences in Examples (1)–(3) all have a score of 1.0 for complex nominals, even though the noun phrase in the first sentence includes both pre- and post-modification, unlike the second and third sentences.

(1)   The green **book** [which is very interesting] was written in 1953.

(2)   The green **book** was written in 1953.

(3)   The book [which is very interesting] was written in 1953.

In summary, this measure of complex nominals is problematic because, among other things, it does not distinguish between pre- and post- modification and between single and multiple modification. Additional problems with this measure include: (1) it is given a label that inaccurately suggests a clear linguistic interpretation, (2) the actual operationalization of the measure differs linguistically from the expectations raised by that label, and (3) it is nearly impossible to evaluate the actual linguistic basis of the measure as applied to specific texts.

While the complex nominals measure is arguably the most linguistically opaque calculation provided by the L2SCA tool, T-unit measures may also be problematic. A T-unit is defined as "one main clause plus any subordinate clause or non-clausal structure that is attached to or embedded in it" (Hunt, 1970: 4). Measures like the mean length of T-unit are computed automatically by available corpus analysis software, and, as a result, they have been used in numerous Second Language Acquisition (SLA) studies of grammatical complexity (see the survey in Housen, De Clercq, Kuiken, & Vedder, 2018). However, as pointed out in Biber et al. (2020), T-unit measures conflate different structural and syntactic characteristics and are thus very difficult to interpret linguistically. Consider the sentences in Examples (4) and (5):

(4)   The thing that we often forget to think about was that the place where people made these interactions musically was out in the fields.

(5)   There is a need for further high-quality research into the association between the experience of stress across a variety of contexts and miscarriage risk.

The first sentence comes from a spoken interview and the second from a medical news article. While both sentences are made up of a single T-unit of the same length, they have very different structural and syntactic characteristics. The sentence in Example (4) is made up of one main clause and four dependent clauses, whereas that in Example (5) is made up of one main clause and several embedded prepositional phrases modifying nouns. If we were to base our analysis solely on the number of T-units or the length of T-units, the two sentences would receive almost identical values. If, by contrast, we were actually to carry out a linguistic analysis of the syntactic makeup of these sentences, we would see that they are vastly different; in fact, the similarities between them do not appear to extend beyond their length. The first sentence uses extensive clausal elaboration, including a *to*-complement clause, a *that*-complement clause, and two relative clauses. In contrast, the second sentence relies on phrasal compression, with multiple phrasal noun modifiers (attributive adjectives, per-modifying nouns, and post-modifying prepositional phrases).

To complicate matters further, the specific measure that we discussed earlier in the section – *complex nominals per T-unit* – is a ratio-based measure, which means that the score is an amalgam of the individual scores from the numerator and the denominator. Thus, any attempt to provide a linguistic interpretation of this score would require a separate evaluation of the score for the number of complex nominals *and* the score for the number of T-units in a text. To illustrate the difficulty of attempting such interpretation, *complex nominals per T-unit* will here be compared to the closely related measure *complex nominals per clause*.

In Larsson and Kaatari (2020), these two measures were found to be strongly correlated in texts written by experts ($r = 0.93$), which meant that their behavior was strongly related. However, this was not the case in the learner texts. Overall, the published writers exhibited a higher average ratio of complex nominals *per clause* than the learners; however, the difference between the published writers and the learners with regard to complex nominals *per T-unit* was minimal. This discrepancy led to a mystery-solving expedition involving investigations of scores for both the numerator and the denominator of this ratio measure.

Due to the complicated nature of ratio measures, there are several possible explanations for the differences noted. For example, all things being equal, fewer dependent clauses in the expert data than in the learner data might possibly explain why the measures were strongly correlated in the expert data, as this would bring scores for clause-based measures closer to those of T-unit-based measures. However, this was not the case in Larsson and Kaatari (2020). After some detective work involving further use of the online mode of the program as well as manual investigation of a subset of the texts, it was instead concluded that the reason for the noted discrepancy seemed to lie primarily in the extent to which structures classified as complex nominals were dispersed evenly across clauses.

However, note that these steps still did not provide a clear answer to the question of how the language of the learners differed from that of the experts, as the complex nominals measure confounds multiple linguistic structures. For this reason, complementary manual, computational, and statistical analyses were carried out to see what was actually causing the differences noted. These analyses showed that the main differences between the experts and the learners lay in the use of prepositional and adjectival modifiers: the experts used a denser style of writing involving more complex noun phrases with pre- and post-modification, in line with previous research on academic writing (e.g. Biber et al., 1999).

The purpose of sharing this experience here is to show that trying to interpret results that stem from automatically calculated measures that are linguistically opaque is a cumbersome and, in many cases, even futile process. Although tools of this kind are very easy to use and give the appearance of carrying out a sophisticated corpus analysis, the measures provided are often linguistically uninterpretable and cannot be evaluated for their linguistic accuracies. Our recommendation is therefore to opt for a simpler analysis if need be, with the primary goal of ensuring an accurate analysis that is directly interpretable relative to the linguistic research questions of interest.

5.3 Conclusion

Ensuring reliable conclusions based on existing corpus-analysis tools usually requires considerable post-processing, for example involving evaluation of accuracy. However, this is made difficult (if not impossible) in cases where no adequate documentation is available and where annotated versions of analyzed texts are not made available to the end-user. If current reporting practices in published corpus linguistic research are any indication, post-processing of the results provided by automatic corpus analysis tools is rarely done. Our main goal in the present section is to encourage researchers to always carry out (and report on) such analyses.

The obvious advantages of using automatic tools are that they are easy, fast, and able to process a large corpus. However, to some extent, the process required to ensure the accuracy and interpretability of corpus linguistic results tempers these benefits. In other words, ensuring accuracy and interpretability may require that the results from an easy, fast, large-scale corpus analysis become only a starting point, not an ending point. Accuracy and interpretability often introduce challenges, decrease speed, and require a smaller-scale study or dataset. Our position is that it is better to analyse a much smaller corpus, and take more time (and more work) to do it, if the end result is findings that are accurate and linguistically meaningful and interpretable.

In general, we should critically examine the tools we use, the results they provide, and the assumptions that those results are based on. Otherwise we risk basing our conclusions on uninformative variables and measures that will seriously impede the interpretability and, thus, the linguistic relevance of the results. Accordingly, we encourage researchers to choose (and/or develop) tools and measures that are linguistically sound and fully documented. In doing so, we can, as a field, work toward more linguistically informative and more robust conclusions.

Key Considerations:
- There is heavy reliance on already existing software tools in the field.
- Many tools offer limited transparency in terms of the accuracy and linguistic basis of automatically computed measures.
- We should aim toward carrying out linguistic analyses that are accurate and interpretable, even if that requires additional time, effort, and skills.

6 The Role of Statistical Analysis in Linguistic Descriptions

6.1 Introduction

As has been argued in the previous sections, decisions about research design – including corpus design, research questions, observational units, variables, and analytical tools – should be linguistically well-founded. Once we have a solid foundation for our study, we can start thinking about which statistical methods to employ.

At a general level, researchers use descriptive statistics (e.g. percent, mean, standard deviation) to quantitatively describe data, and inferential statistics (e.g. chi-square tests, regression analysis) to make inferences about the generalizability of observed patterns vis-à-vis the population that we have sampled from. However, as we shall see, statistical methods (even descriptive ones!) have a tendency to create layers of distance between corpus linguists and the language data in corpora. Sometimes, this distance can help in identifying quantitative patterns in large corpora. However, too much distance between corpus researchers and the actual language in texts – without additional careful analysis – is likely to hinder the linguistic interpretability of the results. Therefore, we need to critically examine our use of statistical methods and how we report on and interpret statistical findings to make sure that our conclusions and discussion are linguistically sound, as discussed in the present section. Specifically, we argue in favor of (1) using appropriate *and* minimally sufficient statistical methods and (2) always making sure to return to the language data to interpret the results of statistical tests. The latter can be achieved by avoiding unnecessary abstractions away from the data, and by carrying out further linguistic analysis after the statistical test itself is completed, to enhance the linguistic interpretability of the results.

The question of what constitutes *appropriate* statistical methods can be approached from several different angles. Introductory textbooks on statistics tend to discuss suitable methods for different types of variable, distribution, and sample. Due to word limitations, however, we will not attempt a comprehensive overview but, rather, focus on some often-overlooked aspects. We begin our discussion by warning against overreliance on a statistical paradigm that permeates almost all corpus linguistics studies, namely the null hypothesis significance testing paradigm. We then broaden the discussion to cover the topic of what constitutes *minimally sufficient* statistical methods. And, finally, we discuss the need to confirm and interpret the results of all statistical analyses through detailed inspection of the targeted linguistic phenomena in particular texts.

Null hypothesis significance testing (NHST) is a statistical paradigm in which differences or relationships in a sample are compared with a null hypothesis to determine whether there is sufficient statistical evidence to reject the null hypothesis and draw a conclusion of statistical "significance". We subscribe to this paradigm any time we use a *p*-value to support conclusions (e.g. using chi-square tests, correlations, or regression analysis). However, what is often overlooked in corpus linguistics studies is the fact that NHST is extremely sensitive to sample size: the larger the sample, the more likely it is to find a statistically significant result. This means that when used for studies involving data from large corpora, which is often the case in our field, NHST will often result in the rejection of the null hypothesis, even for effect sizes that are small and possibly spurious. By extension, overreliance on the NHST paradigm could impede our ability to draw reliable and meaningful conclusions about language use from corpus data.

Put differently, corpus samples are often *overpowered*, meaning that the samples are so large that nearly any measurable difference results in a statistically significant difference (i.e. we reach statistical significance even for very small effect sizes[21] with no practical significance). Put differently, statistical tests based on extremely large samples, which are common in corpus linguistic studies, have *too much* power, leading to an increase in situations where the null hypothesis (of no difference or relationship) is rejected when it is actually true, that is, when there is no difference or relationship in the population. The more technical explanation to support and illustrate these claims can be found in the Appendix.

However, we would like to stress the fact that the most appropriate method for the task at hand should *not* be the most *sophisticated* method we have in our toolbox, unless absolutely necessary. Instead, we should always strive to choose *minimally sufficient* statistical methods, meaning that we should choose tests that are no more nor less sophisticated than the study design requires. The reason for this is twofold: (1) all descriptive and inferential statistical tests force us to abstract away from language to some extent and (2) there is often an inverse relationship between the level of sophistication of the method and the linguistic interpretability of the results. Even simple, seemingly straightforward statistical methods may lead to linguistically questionable conclusions caused by layers of abstraction between the data and the researcher, as illustrated in the example that we look at now (see also the case study in Section 6.3 for an example of an application of a minimally sufficient statistical technique).

---

[21] See, e.g., Brezina (2018: 14 and Section 8.4) for more information about effect sizes in corpus linguistic studies.

The following three contrived datasets (a)–(c) report on the frequency of second-person pronouns in three different 1,000-word text excerpts, all with a mean frequency of 40.2:

a.   40, 40, 40, 40, 41 (mean frequency = 40.2)

b.   20, 30, 40, 50, 61 (mean frequency = 40.2)

c.   10, 10, 10, 10, 161 (mean frequency = 40.2)

The first thing to note is that in summarizing the pronoun frequencies using numbers, we have already abstracted away from language. None of the texts includes exactly 40.2 instances, as pronouns, of course, cannot be fractioned. Second, based on the mean, we might mistakenly draw the conclusion that the data is dispersed (i.e. spread out) similarly and evenly across all three datasets, which is not the case. Third, the mean – or even the raw – frequencies do not provide any information about the functions of those pronouns in the texts; it could be that they serve very different functions in the discourse and that they therefore should not have been grouped together in the first place. Further linguistic analysis would thus be required to learn more (see Section 7).

At the other end of the scale, almost without exception, highly sophisticated methods involve several levels of abstraction away from the actual language data. For example, meeting assumptions of methods such as linear models often requires making changes to the dataset, such as excluding outliers or merging categories with a low number of data points, which may or may not be warranted or advisable from a purely linguistic point of view. They also frequently involve data transformations of different kinds, such as log transformations. Such transformations change the nature of the data, often to a linguistically uninterpretable scale. For example, it is not immediately clear what an increase of five noun phrases per text every two years means when these figures are both reported on a log_e scale. Other examples where the linguistic interpretability of the data becomes obscured and thus difficult to interpret and use to draw conclusions include methods used for identifying collocations such as LogDice (Rychlý, 2008) and frequency measures such as Average Reduced Frequency (ARF) (Savický & Hlaváčová, 2002).

What is to be considered a minimally sufficient method varies depending on the aim and research design; there are, of course, studies for which highly sophisticated methods could be considered minimally sufficient. For example, while some research questions involving comparisons across groups are possible to answer through a *t*-test, others will require a discriminant analysis (see, e.g., Levshina, 2015, for more information about when to use one and not the other). Similarly, for some studies of alternation, reporting simple proportions might suffice, whereas others will require regression analyses and/or random forests (RFs). Some

Table 6.1 Statistical methods at different levels of sophistication grouped by analysis

Sophistication	Group differences	Relationships	Alternation
-	Comparison of means	Bivariate correlations	Proportions
	Effect size	Linear regression	Crosstabs
	t-test; ANOVA	Multiple regression	Logistic regression
	MANOVA	Canonical correlation	Inference trees; Random forests
+	Discriminant analysis	Factor analysis	Multinomial regression

examples of methods for different research goals (group differences, relationships, or alternations) at different levels of sophistication can be found in Table 6.1.

In the first case study (in Section 6.2), we will illustrate the limitations of NHST and the utility of effect sizes for corpus linguistics research. After that, we will turn our attention to the importance of returning to the language data once the tests have been carried out. It is not uncommon in the field for statistical results to be viewed as a conclusion in and of themselves, rather than as a set of findings requiring linguistic interpretation. One reason for this is that reporting of statistical methods and results requires many words of prose, which can limit the remaining space for reporting of qualitative interpretation. However, it is vital that the output of the test is not considered the endpoint of the analysis. Statistical tests cannot replace linguistic analysis; they are, and should remain, tools that assist the researcher in drawing linguistically valid conclusions.

6.2 Case Study 1: Moving Beyond NHST

In the first case study, we apply a traditional NHST approach to compare the rates of occurrence for linguistic features in two corpora. The case study serves to exemplify the potential pitfalls of an overreliance on the results of statistical tests, especially *p*-values. In response to this, we propose that descriptive statistics (including means and standard deviations) and effect sizes are also critically important to consider when analyzing quantitative corpus data. Moreover, we hope to demonstrate the importance of actually examining the use of linguistic features in texts in order to confirm and understand patterns of use.

Our aim in this case study is to investigate whether song lyrics use higher rates of occurrence for features associated with conversation than other registers. The data comes from the Corpus of Online Registers of English (CORE; see Biber & Egbert, 2018). To test this, we compare online song lyrics in CORE ($n = 635$) with all of the other texts in the corpus ($n = 47,936$). We focus on the mean rates of occurrence (normalized per 1,000 words) for 8 linguistic features that have been shown to be strongly associated with the register of conversation (see Biber et al., 1999): first- and second-person pronouns (p. 334), contractions (pp. 1129–32), adverbs (pp. 1044–5), discourse markers (p. 1097), and modals of prediction, possibility, and necessity (p. 1044).

The first – and often *only* – step in a traditional approach is to run a statistical test to determine whether the means for the two groups are significantly different. Based on this, we used R (R Core Team, 2020) to run a series of eight independent samples t-tests to compare song lyrics to other online registers. In order to adjust for multiple comparisons, we adopted a conservative Bonferroni adjusted alpha of .00625 (.05 / 8). The results show that all eight of the features were "significantly" different between the two groups, even using our conservative Bonferroni-adjusted alpha (see Table 6.2). In fact, it can be noted that, for all of these features, the p-values were so miniscule that any reasonable alpha would result in a rejection of the null hypothesis. The smallest p-value that R reported was $p = 1.82e^{-115}$, meaning that the 182 is preceded by 115 zeros. It is important to remember, however, that p-values cannot be interpreted in terms of the magnitude of the effect (i.e. difference or association). Thus, for our purposes here (and

Table 6.2 p-values for linguistic features (based on t tests comparing song lyrics to other online registers)

Variable	p
1st person pronouns	$1.82e^{-115}$
2nd person pronouns	$2.00e^{-67}$
Contractions	$1.47e^{-77}$
Adverbs	0.000356
Discourse markers	0.003908
Modals of prediction	$2.85e^{-19}$
Modals of possibility	$3.25e^{-13}$
Modals of necessity	0.005749

Table 6.3 Means and standard deviations for eight linguistic features (song lyrics and other online registers)

Variable	Song lyrics		Other online	
	M	*SD*	*M*	*SD*
1st person pronouns	79.28	45.44	27.94	23.71
2nd person pronouns	39.95	34.88	12.75	17.48
Contractions	42.45	28.11	18.43	12.37
Adverbs	37.96	23.41	34.62	12.78
Discourse markers	1.04	3.38	0.65	1.52
Modals of prediction	13.54	15.42	7.86	6.82
Modals of possibility	10.29	12.00	6.74	5.59
Modals of necessity	3.14	7.42	2.33	3.09

within the frequentist NHST paradigm generally), the relative size of the *p*-value does not matter, only whether it is below or above our a priori alpha of .00625.

It is not uncommon for corpus-based studies to stop at this point and draw conclusions on the basis of the "significant" differences revealed by the *p*-values that are below our alpha of $p < .00625$. However, this approach can lead to results that are uninformative, at best, or completely misleading, at worst. Thus, we propose that researchers treat the results of statistical tests as a starting point, not an ending point. While it is true that researchers often report informative descriptive statistics (e.g. means, standard deviations), often in tables or parentheticals, it seems to be much more common to rely on and interpret *p*-values in the analysis.

In the present study, if we explore our results further by going back to descriptive statistics, we find that some of these mean differences are extremely small (see Table 6.3), even though they are clearly "significant" (see Table 6.2). Take, for example, the difference between the means for adverbs in the two groups: 37.96 in song lyrics and 34.62 in other online registers. This reveals that, on average, song lyrics use 3.34 more adverbs per 1,000 words than other online registers. Similarly, there is an even smaller mean difference in the use of modals of necessity, with song lyrics using just .81 more modals of necessity per 1,000 words. A close qualitative analysis of the texts in these groups confirms that these differences are essentially undetectable and, for practical, descriptive purposes, insignificant.

We can also go a step further toward understanding the magnitude of these differences by computing Cohen's *d*, which is an effect size calculated by dividing the difference between two group means by their pooled standard deviation. Unlike *p*-values, effect sizes quantify the magnitude of the difference between groups. The Cohen's *d* results are reported in Table 6.4 below, ranked highest to lowest. If we use the benchmarks proposed by Cohen (1977) – 0.2:

Table 6.4 Cohen's *d* values for eight
linguistic features (between song
lyrics and other online registers)

Variable	d
1st person pronouns	1.42
Contractions	1.11
2nd person pronouns	0.99
Modals of prediction	0.48
Modals of possibility	0.38
Adverbs	0.18
Discourse markers	0.15
Modals of necessity	0.14

small; 0.5: medium; 0.8: large – then we can see that the first three features achieved large effect sizes, the next three features achieved small effect sizes, and the last three features show only negligible effects.

These results are important because they reveal weaknesses of NHST-type tests when applied to large samples. As we have discussed, all else being equal, *p*-values will always decrease as sample size increases. With the extremely large sample sizes used in corpus linguistics, this can mean that even negligible effects (i.e. results that are practically insignificant) can be flagged as statistically significant. As mentioned, another weakness of *p*-values is that they cannot be interpreted as a continuous measure of effect size. Some erroneously believe that a lower *p*-value means that there is a stronger effect, but that is simply untrue: *p*-values merely provide information that allows us to make a binary distinction between *significant* and *not significant*. As we have shown here, it is quite possible – and arguably quite common in corpus linguistics – to achieve low *p*-values, even for effects that are very small.

We hope to have shown in this case study that statistical tests of significance should not be used as the sole basis for drawing conclusions about the importance or magnitude of statistical differences (or relationships). We advocate for an approach in which researchers *always* examine (1) descriptive statistics and (2) effect sizes. Some researchers may also feel inclined to apply a statistical test of significance and interpret a *p*-value. There is nothing inherently wrong with this, but we believe that this step should be viewed as optional and limited in the amount of information that it can provide; statistical tests of significance and *p*-values should not be used exclusively or in place of descriptives, effect sizes, and analysis of actual texts.

6.3 Case Study 2: On the Importance of Staying Close to the Language Data

The aim of the second case study is to highlight the pitfall of treating statistical results as the endpoint of the analysis, even when using sophisticated (yet minimally sufficient) statistical methods.

In this case study, we report on a re-analysis of a subset of the data from Larsson, Callies, Hasselgård, Laso, Van Vuuren, Verdaguer, & Paquout (2020), namely Swedish and British university students' written data from the Varieties of English for Specific Purposes Database (VESPA) and the British Academic Written English Corpus (BAWE), respectively. Specifically, the case study seeks to investigate what linguistic and extralinguistic variables are most useful for distinguishing between adverb positions in spoken and written production by non-native speakers and native speakers of English. Fifteen epistemic adverbs were included in the analysis: *maybe, perhaps, probably, surely, clearly, actually, apparently, definitely, certainly, evidently, obviously, possibly, really, of course,* and *simply.* Hasselgård's (2010: 41–53; based on Quirk, Greenbaum, Leech, & Svartvik, 1985: 490–501) classification of clausal positions was used; this is outlined in Table 6.5.[22]

Table 6.5 Clausal positions (adapted from Hasselgård 2010: 42)

Position	Definition	Example
Initial (I)	The position "before the obligatory element in the clause"	*In short,* **perhaps** *there are alternative routes* (LING012-03).
Medial 1 (M1)	The position "between the subject and any part of the verb phrase"	*The experimenter* **actually** *uses direct reported speech to introduce the receiver's prior imagery* (LING010-05).
Medial 2 (M2)	The position "after the (first) auxiliary but before the main verb"	*Readers may* **actually** *focus more on modeling global text content* (LING004-04).
Medial 3 (M3)	The position "between the verb phrase and some other obligatory element, viz. an object, a predicative, or an obligatory adverbial"	*Empathy is* **surely** *as important a human capability as choice* (LING011-02).

[22] Although adverbs of course can be placed in clause-final position too, our results show that this position is very infrequently used in written data: only three instances were found in the data used for the present case study. This position will therefore not be considered here.

The following extralinguistic and linguistic variables were coded for and included in this case study: native-speaker status (non-native speaker vs. native-speaker students), presence/absence of auxiliary, presence/absence of other adverbials in the clause, verb type (copular/linking, intransitive, monotransitive, ditransitive, complex transitive), adverb (the fifteen adverbs included), clause type (main clause vs. subordinate clause), and type of subject (zero subject, pronoun, noun phrase, clausal).

To make sense of all of the variables and their relative importance for the positional distribution of the adverbs, a conditional inference tree (CIT) was fitted onto the data.[23] Since our goal here is not to provide a comprehensive introduction to CITs, readers are referred to works such as Gries (forthcoming) and Levshina (forthcoming) for a more detailed description. Nonetheless, a brief overview of CITs will be presented here, as an elementary understanding of this technique is likely to be necessary in order to be able to follow along with the points made in this case study.

CITs belong to the family of recursive partitioning methods, for which a series of splits are made to the data such that the observations in each resulting category are maximally similar (see Levshina, forthcoming). Using the *ctree* function from the *party* package (Strobl, Boulesteix, Kneib, Augustin, & Zeileis, 2008), we fitted a CIT onto the present dataset; the tree can be found in Figure 6.1.

The top split represents the most important predictor, followed by the second most important predictor, given the first predictor. CITs can thus provide an overview of high-order interactions. As can be seen from Figure 6.1, the presence of one or several auxiliary (AUX_YN) is the most important predictor, followed by verb type (VERB_TYPE) and clause type (CLAUSE_TYPE), respectively. In more detail, starting from the top, we can see that if there is no auxiliary (AUX_YN: NO) but there is a linking verb (VERB_TYPE: L), then the M3 position is predicted (i.e. the graphs in both terminal nodes show a clear preference for M3). However, the final split (SUBJ_TYPE) tells us that there is a slight (albeit still statistically significant) preference for the I position for clauses with no subjects (Z) or a nominal subject (NP), compared to clauses with a pronominal (P) or clausal (C) subject. We can also note in passing that native-speaker status proved to be an important factor in this dataset (in fact, a separate analysis showed that this variable did not have any discriminatory power).

---

[23] As CITs are based on a random sample of observations and variables from the original dataset, it is preferable to run an RF instead, as the latter is made up of averaged predictions of a large number of CITs, thus providing more stable and accurate predictions than CITs (Gries, forthcoming). For the sake of simplicity, however, we will not go on to fit an RF in this case study.

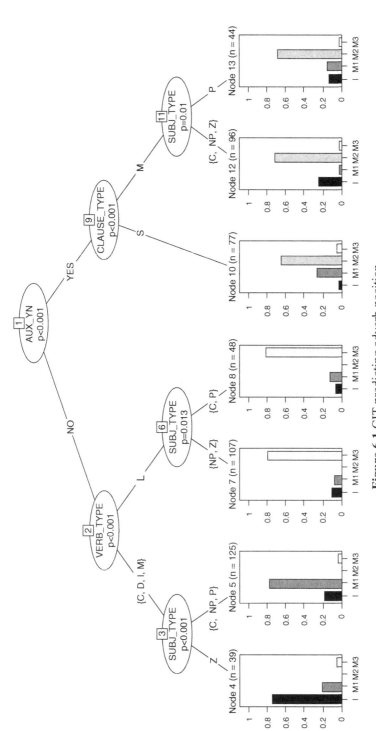

Figure 6.1 CIT-predicting adverb position

Returning to the goals of the present case study, the sophistication of this method may make it seem as if it does not adhere to the recommendation of always trying to use minimally sufficient statistical techniques. However, while it is true that CIT analysis is a sophisticated method, there are several reasons why it would be deemed minimally sufficient and more appropriate than alternative techniques. For example, it would have been much too time-consuming (and perhaps even impossible) to try to make sense of all the variables, their relative importance, and their interrelationships by relying only on descriptive statistics or simpler monofactorial hypothesis-testing techniques that rely on pair-wise comparisons. Furthermore, unlike regression models, CITs can be used in cases where general regression assumptions, such as the assumptions of homoscedasticity and linearity, are not met. In more detail, CITs (and RFs) can be used for studies such as this in which variables can be expected to be correlated or where the number of observations is relatively small in relation to the number of variables (Levshina, forthcoming).

In fact, no assumptions (of the kind we are used to from working with logistic regression models) need to be met when fitting CITs or RFs (Levshina, forthcoming),[24] which is helpful if the goal is to avoid abstracting away from the data. Since a common reason for applying data transformation techniques (e.g. log transformations) is to try to meet assumptions of a statistical test, the fact that this is not necessary means that, in using a CIT, we can work with the original variables instead of trying to explain the effect of variables that are linguistically more opaque. In addition, the output of CITs is conceptually easier to interpret and in some cases more intuitive than the output of other techniques (compare Gries, forthcoming; Baayen, Janda, Nesset, Endresen, & Makarova, 2013), which increases the interpretability of the results and thus, arguably, lowers the risk of misinterpretation.

We might be tempted to stop here and have this plot and the discussion of these findings be the endpoint of the study. However, doing so would leave several questions of linguistic importance unanswered. Most notably, if we do not return to the data, we are not able to understand what the distributional preferences of the adverbs actually mean linguistically (e.g. does a less pronounced preference for any given position mean that such uses are marked or just less common?). Furthermore, while Figure 6.1 gives us the overview of the interactions, it may be helpful to look at individual variables to better understand the results. We will here take a closer look at the cumulative frequencies of the variable that the CIT identified as most important, *auxiliary: yes/no*, to illustrate these points (see Larsson et al., 2020, for other examples along with information about the dispersion across texts).

---

[24] However, see Levshina (forthcoming) for a discussion of the independence of observations.

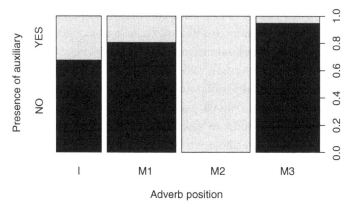

Figure 6.2 Cumulative frequency of presence/absence of auxiliary across the four adverb positions

The distribution, shown in the mosaic plot in Figure 6.2, displays clear trends across the adverb positions for *auxiliary: yes/no*. The size of the bars of a mosaic plot provides information about the relative frequency of each of the variables on the *y* and *x* axes.

As presence of an auxiliary is a prerequisite of the M2 position, the perfect prediction for M2 should come as no surprise (i.e. 100 percent of tokens where the adverb is found in the M2 position have at least one auxiliary in the verb phrase); a corpus example showing the adverb simply in M2 position can be found in (6). However, when we take a closer look at the data, we can see that many of the instances where the adverb has been placed in M1 (7) or M3 (8) position would actually be considered marked, which suggests that the most expected position for adverbs is the M2 position when there is at least one auxiliary in the verb phrase. We can also see that the clause-initial position includes many unmarked and grammatical exceptions to this preference, as exemplified in (9). Note here that it would not have been possible to arrive at these conclusions if our analysis had been based solely on the output of the CIT, which highlights the importance of returning to the data to perform complementary analyses.

(6)   Another explanation could **simply** be that this kind of initialism originates from the Internet (LING0019).

(7)   ? This **perhaps** might have implications in terms of assessment (LING3118b).

(8)   ? This study would uncover **perhaps** an unrepresentative amount of words with a certain type of meaning (LING6061b).

(9)   **Perhaps** a different type of community should take part in the investigation (LING0013).

This case study demonstrates that statistical techniques cannot provide a substitute for linguistic analysis; they should instead be used as a tool that informs the description and the interpretation of linguistic results. We also exemplified how the choice of method indirectly or directly can lead researchers further away from the data and the analysis of language, and how we need to return to the language data to obtain a more complete picture of the results.

6.4 Conclusion

Language is, and should remain, the primary focus of corpus linguistic investigations. There is no denying that statistical methods are very useful – and oftentimes necessary – for detecting tendencies that might otherwise go unnoticed. However, sophisticated statistical methods often create layers of distance between corpus researchers and the language data they aim to describe, which is likely to negatively affect the linguistic validity of the results. Put differently, any kind of abstraction away from the language data comes with an opportunity cost because it increases the risk of obtaining linguistically uninterpretable results, which, in turn, is more likely to lead to misinterpretations and unsatisfactory conclusions.

In order to avoid abstracting away from the language data, we should always attempt to use minimally sufficient statistical techniques that are well-aligned with the research question we have in mind. We believe that moving toward acceptance of minimally sufficient statistical methods will help us, as a field, to avoid losing sight of the object of our primary training: language itself. To this end, regardless of the degree of sophistication in statistical methods, it is imperative to return to descriptive statistics and effect sizes to explain and interpret observed patterns. Finally, it is crucial that researchers also examine the actual linguistic patterns in the texts themselves to explain and interpret the numeric trends observed. This type of qualitative linguistic analysis is the focus of Section 7.

Key Considerations:

- Sophisticated statistical methods often force researchers to abstract away very far from the language data.
- It is important to employ minimally sufficient statistical methods to remain as close as possible to the language data.
- Overreliance on NHST for large samples is problematic in corpus linguistics, given its sensitivity to n size.
- NHST should always be complemented by consideration of descriptive statics and effect sizes.
- We have to make a conscious effort to return to the language data to interpret numeric results.

7 Interpreting Quantitative Results

7.1 Introduction

In this section, we pull together many of the themes of previous sections, ultimately arguing that linguistics is done by linguists, not by computers. Computers can aid linguists in countless ways, but they cannot replace the vital role of the linguist in corpus linguistics, which is, among other things, to interpret quantitative findings from corpus data as meaningful patterns of language use. When quantitative methods are presented without sufficient linguistic interpretation, they are not really useful for answering important questions about language. In contrast, when quantitative results are coupled with sound qualitative linguistic interpretation, patterns in the form of mere numbers can be brought to life in ways that provide important insights into language use, variation, development, and change. There are many sources of information at the linguist's disposal that can be used to carry out qualitative analysis and interpretation of quantitative corpus data. In this brief introduction, we discuss three of these sources of information: (1) linguistic context, (2) text-external context, and (3) linguistic principles and theories.

Linguistic context is available in abundance in corpus data. Texts are rich sources of linguistic information regarding the contexts in which structures, patterns, and words actually occur. Fortunately for corpus linguists, this linguistic context can often be extracted and analyzed with ease by using nothing more than a concordancing software package to generate a list of concordance lines for a pattern or word of interest. Alternatively, researchers can use quantitative methods, such as dimension scores from multidimensional (MD) analysis or prototypical texts from a tool like ProtAnt (see Anthony & Baker, 2015), to identify a subset of texts for closer evaluation and analysis. In either case, concordance lines and texts can then serve as the basis for qualitative research and sources for illustrative examples of quantitative patterns. When accounting for linguistic context in quantitative corpus research, the key is to retrace our steps to get back to the actual language contained in the corpus. Methods for using linguistic context will be illustrated in the case study in Section 7.2.

Text-external context can come from many sources. One source is metadata about the corpus texts themselves regarding the source of the text, including year of production/publication, speaker/writer demographics, and publication information. Another source of text-external context is the situational characteristics of texts within or across registers, which can be ascertained through a situational analysis (see Biber & Conrad, 2019). Text-external context can be found in prior findings from research in other disciplines, including history, sociology, political science, psychology, and education. Finally, researchers can use methodological triangulation to gather additional data regarding the texts or language in the corpus using methods such as brain imaging (e.g. MRI, EEG), sociolinguistic instruments (e.g. questionnaires, surveys), psycholinguistic methods (e.g. sentence completion tasks, lexical decision tasks), and language testing (e.g. test taker scores, text difficulty scores), among others (see Egbert & Baker, 2019). These sources of data can help linguists to interpret quantitative findings that emerge from quantitative corpus linguistics. The usefulness of text-external context will be highlighted in the case study in Section 7.3.

Finally, quantitative corpus linguists can draw on existing principles and theories of linguistics in order to make sense of their findings. A good example of a healthy relationship between linguistic theory and quantitative corpus linguistics is usage-based linguistics. Usage-based linguistics "explores how we learn language from our experience of language" (Ellis, 2019). The data for language users' experiences typically comes from quantitative corpus linguistics. This data is then interpreted in light of current research and theories of language learning, and the data may influence the theories moving forward. There are many other examples of theoretical approaches that can serve as the basis for interpreting corpus linguistic findings, and that, in turn, can further inform the theory.

The sources of information we have mentioned here – linguistic context, text-external context, and linguistic principles and theories – represent only some of the approaches that a corpus linguist can use to interpret quantitative linguistic patterns. Regardless of the source of the information, we cannot overstate how important it is for corpus linguists not to lose sight of their role as linguists throughout all stages of quantitative corpus research. It can be tempting to step back and let quantitative results "speak for themselves," but we urge corpus researchers to continue to be linguists long after the computer has produced quantitative/statistical results. While it can be useful at times for corpus linguists to put on a "computer programmer hat" or a "statistician hat," we hope that these hats will not replace the one that should always be worn no matter what – the "linguist hat".

We now turn to three case studies to demonstrate ways in which qualitative linguistic analysis can augment quantitative linguistic findings. Case Study 1 (in Section 7.2) demonstrates the importance of accounting for linguistic context when interpreting collocational patterns. Case Study 2 (in Section 7.3) presents a detailed account of the process of interpreting a dimension from an MD analysis. MD analysis is a quantitative method for identifying linguistically interpretable dimensions of language variation based on underlying co-occurrence patterns among features. The particular dimension of interest is one that required careful accounting of linguistic context and text-external context, in the form of situational characteristics of the texts, before it could be fully interpreted.

Case Study 3 (in Section 7.4) revisits the quantitative findings from a previous study in which the qualitative interpretation provided was limited. We carry out a more thorough and complete linguistic analysis, drawing heavily on text-external context in the form of research from other disciplines and, to a lesser degree, linguistic context.

7.2 Case Study 1: Interpreting Collocational Patterns

In this brief case study, we aim to show the importance of qualitative analysis in the interpretation of collocation results. We pick up where Case Study 1 in Section 4.2 left off, with the list of the ten most frequent content word collocates for *man* and *woman* that occur one word to the left of the node word (see Table 7.1). In the results reported in Section 4.2, we saw that six of the ten words are in both lists, that is, the same for *man* and *woman*, and four words are unique to one list. We focus here on the words that are unique to one list (bolded in Table 7.1).

Table 7.1 Top 10 content word collocates for *man* and *woman* (one word to the left; based on frequency)

Preceding word	Top 10 most frequent with *man*	Top 10 most frequent with *woman*
young	***	***
old	***	***
unidentified	***	***
black	***	***
white	***	***
older	***	***
good	***	
big	***	
dead	***	
little	***	
beautiful		***
pregnant		***
American		***
elderly		***

Table 7.2 Frequencies for three semantic patterns for *dead man*

Pattern	Examples	Frequency
Literal/specific deceased male	The **dead man** has been identified as twenty-five-year-old Roosevelt Rene.	69
Literal/generic deceased male	[A]nd wouldn't see the funny side to his ending up with a **dead man** as companion in his "hour of need".	24
Metaphorical use	It was then Garraty realized that he should have been a **dead man**, and he was one, somewhere deep down.	7
TOTAL		100

For the sake of space,[25] we will select only one word from the four words unique to each node word for further qualitative analysis: *dead* for *man* and *American* for *woman*. For both of these two collocations, we manually coded the first 100 concordance lines into categories based on relevant semantic patterns. Before carrying out the qualitative coding, we hypothesized that *dead man* would most often be a metaphorical use, as in "If you're late again, you're a *dead man*". And we hypothesized that *American woman* would frequently refer to the title of the Lenny Kravitz song. As you will see, we were wrong on both accounts.

After an initial review of the *dead man* collocations, we determined that there were three major semantic patterns: (1) literal/specific deceased male, (2) literal/generic deceased male, and (3) metaphorical use. The frequency breakdown of the first 100 concordance lines into these categories can be seen in Table 7.2.

The overwhelming majority (93 percent) of the cases were literal uses of *dead*, with most of them references to a specific deceased male. It is worth noting, though, that there are strong register patterns here: fifty-one of the sixty-nine literal uses (74 percent) were from fiction writing. Ten of the twenty-four instances of *dead man* in the literal/generic category were part of the title of a movie or song. Our hypothesis regarding metaphorical uses of *dead man* was wrong, at least for this sample.

We similarly coded the top 100 instances of *American woman* according to four salient semantic patterns: (1) minority groups, (2) "generic" – women who are American, (3) Sally Ride, and (4) titles, as shown in Table 7.3.

---

[25] These patterns would deserve much more in-depth analyses in a book- or article-length treatment. Due to the wide range of topics addressed in this Element, we are limited in the amount of analysis we can present from any one case study or example.

Table 7.3 Frequencies for three semantic patterns for *American woman*

Pattern	Examples	Frequency
Minority groups	And as an African **American woman**, she's no stranger to people labeling her as angry.	47
"Generic" – women who are American	Doesn't every **American woman** aspire to marry an attorney?	42
Sally Ride	Among them was Sally Ride, who became the first **American woman** to fly in space in 1983.	6
Titles	Out in the bar they're playing **"American Woman"**.	5
TOTAL		100

Our hypothesis about the song title "American Woman" was wrong. The vast majority of the collocates were indeed examples of a speaker or writer characterizing a woman as American. However, the coding revealed an interesting pattern. The largest category was that of minority groups. Nearly half of the cases of *American woman* are actually references to membership in a more specific minority group, including *Native American, African American, Asian American, black American, Dominican American, Muslim American, Arab American,* and *Vietnamese American.* In many cases, these are likely to be two-word formulaic units that are used primarily to describe the ethnic group membership of a woman, not her status as an American.

It is interesting to note that, based on these findings, it is more common to describe *men* as *dead* and *women* as *American.* However, as has been shown, collocation lists are not an end in themselves. They simply do not include enough linguistic context to provide the basis for conclusions that are accurate and complete. For example, knowing that *dead* was a collocate for *man* did not help us to detect the difference between specific versus generic uses of a word, or between literal versus metaphorical meanings. We were surprised to find that *dead man* most often referred to a literal deceased male. This may be because there are more newsworthy deaths of males than females. Likewise, in the case of *American woman*, the collocation had the potential to be misleading as it masked the larger multi-word units related to minority group membership. It is not clear why it is so common for women to be described based on their minority group status.

The results presented here thus illustrate the importance of further analysis beyond frequency-based results, adding layers of information about the way *dead man* and *American woman* are used in the corpus. Regardless of whether other researchers would have adopted our same hypotheses, without a close qualitative analysis, some of these patterns would likely have been missed entirely. In other words, it is unlikely that a researcher's intuitions about the use of these collocations would have provided them with the rich information we gain from even a cursory qualitative analysis. This begs the question: How much qualitative analysis is sufficient and appropriate? The simple answer is that this depends on the research question. We would simply add that, in our experience, most studies fall on the side of not including enough qualitative analysis to answer the research questions posed. These implications extend to other words lists used in corpus linguistics, including word frequency lists, keyword lists, and lists of words that fill particular syntactic positions (e.g. verbs in verb-argument constructions (VACs)).

7.3 Case Study 2: Interpreting Dimensions of Linguistic Variation

The goal of this case study is to demonstrate how linguistic and text-external sources can be used to interpret complex linguistic patterns in corpus data, namely in an MD analysis. MD analysis is a methodology that relies on linguistic co-occurrence patterns among linguistic features to reveal under-lying dimensions of linguistic variation that are functionally interpretable (see Biber, 1984, 1988). MD analysis is a classic example of a complex statistical technique that can create distance between a researcher and lan-guage data (see Section 6). Thus, the researcher must be vigilant to ensure that the analysis of language remains the central goal throughout all stages of the analysis.

In this case study, we revisit the functional interpretation of one of the dimensions from Egbert (2014, 2015) to demonstrate the importance of lan-guage analysis in this process. The MD analysis in those studies was performed on a corpus of 150 excerpts taken from academic writing in three publication types (journal articles, university textbooks, popular academic writing) and two disciplines (biology, history). The factor analysis was based on a set of fifty-six linguistic features that were carefully selected based on their documented or hypothesized functions in this discourse domain. Five factors were extracted. In this case study, we will discuss the functional interpretations for the second factors, with the goal of demonstrating the importance of careful language analysis in this process.

In some cases, the features that load (positively or negatively) on a dimension can appear on the surface to be readily interpretable, especially if the researcher is experienced with MD analysis or if similar co-occurrence patterns have emerged in a previous MD study. However, it is always advisable to return to the language in actual texts, even if only to confirm that the hypothesized functions are indeed the most appropriate interpretation. The same co-occurrence patterns in two different corpora can, and often do, have functional interpretations that are quite different. Even individual linguistic features are not monofunctional; their functions can be determined only in the context of actual language use. For example, first-person pronouns have functions in interactive discourse, stance expression, and personal narrative, among other functions. Knowing that personal pronouns are relatively frequent is not enough to draw conclusions about how they are functioning in language use.

To complicate matters further in MD analysis, functional interpretation becomes even more complex when it is based on co-occurrence patterns among multiple linguistic features. Throughout the process of carrying out an MD analysis, there are several critical decision points that cannot be success-fully navigated without a sound understanding of the language patterns under investigation. One such decision point in MD analysis involves how to interpret and label each of the dimensions extracted from the factor analysis. The main challenge in carrying out that interpretation is that MD dimensions are several steps removed from the actual language in the texts, as seen in the left-hand side of Figure 7.1.

While it is possible for a researcher to retrace steps 1–5 in reverse order to make their way back to the actual texts, there is a better way, which is to use dimension scores and register patterns to return to the language use (see Figure 7.2). This method includes (1) the computation of scores for each dimension on each text, (2) statistical analysis of register patterns, and (3) the interpretation of those register patterns in texts. We demonstrate this approach, applied to Egbert's (2014, 2015) Dimension 2.

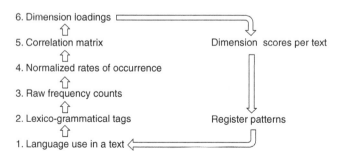

Figure 7.1 Using dimension scores and register patterns in dimension
interpretation

Table 7.4 Linguistic features that loaded on Dimension 2

Dimension 2

Positive features:
Nouns and pronouns: demonstrative pronouns (.40), concrete (.30), pronoun "it" (.34)
Verbs: possibility, permission, and ability modals (.67), verb BE (.59), prediction modals (.38)
Verb phrase: present tense (.73)
Adjectives: predicative adjectives (.53)
Clauses marking stance: non-finite *to*-clauses controlled by stance adjectives (.68), *that*-clauses controlled by attitudinal adjectives (.57)
Lexical features: academic lexical bundles (.58)

Negative features:
NONE

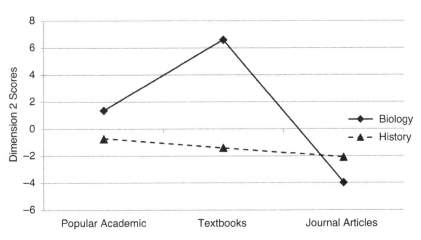

Figure 7.2 Interaction plot for Dimension 2

Dimension 2 did not have a close analog in any previously published MD study. This dimension has no negative features, and the shared function of the positive loading features was not immediately apparent (see Table 7.4). In this case, the two primary situational variables are publication type (popular academic, textbooks, journal articles) and discipline (biology, history). The more we know about the situational characteristics of each of these publication types and disciplines, as well as key differences among them, the better we are able to understand and interpret functional language use as quantified by the dimension scores and exemplified in texts.

The interaction plot in Figure 7.2 displays the mean for each of the six registers in the corpus. The most striking pattern is that university textbooks in biology have much higher Dimension 2 scores than any of the other groups. In fact, the only other register with a positive Dimension 2 score is popular academic books in biology. This pattern begged a closer investigation of the use of the positive loading features on this dimension in biology university textbooks.

Excerpt 3, taken from a university textbook in biology, demonstrates the co-occurrence patterns of the positive features of Dimension 2. Modals of possibility, permission, and ability and modals of prediction are highlighted in **bold**; BE verbs are in SMALL CAPS; predicative adjectives are underlined; demonstrative and "it" pronouns are double underlined; and present tense verb phrases are *italicized*. It can be seen in this short excerpt how these features are used, in combination, to define and evaluate new concepts. The pronouns are used as referents for the concepts being defined and evaluated. The different forms of BE are used as stative verbs and the modal *can* describes and evaluates the characteristics of the concepts being defined.

> **Excerpt 3**   Besides a cellular response to infection, we *ARE* also protected by our complement system. This *IS* a collection of proteins that *act* together to produce a cascade response. Even a weak signal **can** BE amplified in this way to elicit a strong response. The complement system *has* two major effects. It **can** *act* directly on invading microbes or it **can** *act* in association with antibody to cause cell lysis. It *does* so by *puncturing* holes in the microbial cell membrane. [TB_BI_15, D2 score: 16.32]

Once these patterns in biology textbooks were explored further, it became clear why this register received the highest Dimension 2 score by such a large margin. Whereas history writing deals more with events, peoples, records, and artifacts than it does with concepts, biology writing relies heavily on specialized terminology and concepts. Thus, we would expect higher Dimension 2 scores in biology. Additionally, we would expect pedagogical writing within biology to use more language associated with defining concepts than popular writing because one of the major goals of pedagogical writing is to transmit information regarding new concepts in a way that students can understand and retain. Journal articles in biology are written to discipline experts who already know most of the technical terms, and popular academic writing avoids new terms and concepts entirely, whenever possible. Once all of these considerations were accounted for and analyzed within texts in the corpus, Dimension 2 was assigned the label "Definition and Evaluation of New Concepts".

Had we not accounted for several factors, including the statistical results, language use in actual texts, and knowledge of the situational context of the disciplines under investigation, our functional interpretation of this dimension would have been incomplete or inaccurate. Although this case study focused on MD analysis, the methods of qualitative analysis demonstrated here could be applied, with minor adaptations, to the functional interpretation of individual linguistic features, or to linguistic patterns that emerge in other multivariate analyses (e.g. cluster analysis, discriminant analysis).

7.4 Case Study 3: Interpreting Diachronic Trends

The purpose of this case study is to demonstrate the importance of carrying out qualitative language analysis in historical corpus linguistics in order to interpret diachronic trends in corpus linguistic data. Egbert and Davies (2019) investigated diachronic change in meaning relationships that can exist between the two nouns in noun+noun (NN) sequences. They identified twelve meaning relationship categories (see Table 7.5).

The first step in this study was to identify the most frequent NN sequences from a historical corpus. The Corpus of Historical American English (COHA) was used in this study. In line with our discussion in Section 2, the choice of corpus should be based on a thorough evaluation of the corpus and the extent to which its contents align with the target discourse domain. COHA was divided into 6 time periods (1810–1849; 1850–1889; 1890–1929; 1930–1959; 1960–1989; 1990–2009), and the 400 most frequent NNs from each of the 6 time periods were included in the dataset. This resulted in the 1,535 most frequent NN types. Frequency data (per million words) for each decade was recorded for each NN sequence.

Egbert and Davies then developed and piloted a new instrument to make it possible for human raters to classify NN sequences into these meaning relationship categories. Using this instrument, each of the 1,535 NN sequences was coded by 4 independent coders recruited through Amazon's Mechanical Turk. This method resulted in acceptable levels of agreement, and they were able to assign a single semantic category to 64 percent (n = 974) of the NN sequences in the dataset.

The subset of NNs that met the agreement criteria was included in this study. These NN sequences, along with normed rates of occurrence (per million words) for each of the six major COHA time periods, were stored in a spreadsheet. The data was used to compute corpus frequency means for each of the twelve semantic categories in each time period. The means were used to measure diachronic change in the use of the twelve semantic categories across the six time periods in the corpus.

Table 7.5 Semantic categories of NNs, with rephrased sentences and examples

Category	Rephrased sentence	Examples
Composition	N2 is made from N1.	*brass button* *grape juice*
Time	N2 is found or takes place at the time of N1.	*autumn leaf* *summer air*
Location	N2 is found or takes place at the location of N1.	*street light* *mountain stream*
Partitive	N2 is one of the parts that makes up an N1.	*shirt collar* *television screen*
Specialization	N2 is a person. N1 is what he/she specializes in.	*sales manager* *construction worker*
Institution	N2 is an institution. N1 is the type of institution.	*police department* *law school*
Identity	A/an N1 N2 is a/an N1 and it is also a/an N2.	*patron saint* *minority student*
Source	N1 is the source of the N2.	*farm income* *man power*
Purpose	N1 is the purpose or use for N2.	*assault weapon* *operating room*
Topic	N1 is the topic of the N2.	*tax law* *science fiction*
Process	N2 is a process related to N1.	*air conditioning* *population growth*
Ownership	N2 is owned by N1.	*enemy plane* *family mansion*

These results revealed that all of the semantic categories increased over time. However, the rate of increase varied by semantic category. These references to frequency are meant to be relative to the other semantic categories in the data. Egbert and Davies identified three underlying patterns:

1. Frequent → Frequent
   a. Location
   b. Composition
2. Infrequent → Infrequent
   a. Time
   b. Identity
   c. Partitive
   d. Topic

  e. Source
  f. Ownership
3. Infrequent → Frequent
  a. Institution
  b. Specialization
  c. Purpose
  d. Process

In the present analysis, we focus on Pattern 3 with the goal of using socio-historical context, along with qualitative corpus data, to interpret this trend. Although Egbert and Davies offer some preliminary commentary on possible qualitative interpretations, this is insufficient to fully contextualize and interpret the results they observed. In this brief case study, we aim to more fully interpret the quantitative patterns in the use of NN sequences over time. In doing so, we hope to illustrate how additional linguistic analysis and qualitative interpretation can bring to light important discoveries about language use.

Pattern 3 contains four semantic categories of NN sequence that saw the largest increases in frequency over time: institution, specialization, purpose, and process. We focus here on institution and specialization, the two semantic categories within this pattern that experienced the largest increases over time. The quantitative trends for these two categories can be seen in Figure 7.3.

Egbert and Davies posit that there are two potential causes for this pattern. The first cause is "increasing specialization in scientific disciplines, government, commerce, job descriptions, and technology" and the second cause is "a shift toward increased economy in the language that manifests itself in the use of compressed phrases rather than elaborated clauses, especially in writing". We

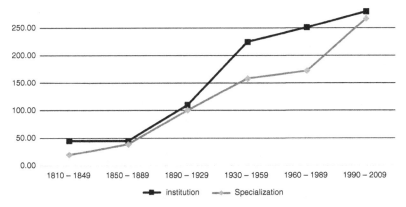

Figure 7.3 Diachronic change in the semantic categories within Pattern 3 – Infrequent → Frequent

Table 7.6 Ten most frequent NN sequences in the Institution and Specialization categories in the first and last time periods

	1810–1849	1990–2009
Institution	state government	law enforcement
	slave trade	stock market
	state legislature	grocery store
	post office	insurance company
	state court	law firm
	executive department	school system
	grammar school	oil company
	animal kingdom	law school
	judiciary department	radio station
	church government	gas station
Specialization	war chief	police officer
	district attorney	school counselor
	bosom friend	school student
	police officer	role model
	business man	government official
	executive magistrate	graduate student
	town clerk	education teacher
	field officer	district attorney
	mound builder	defense attorney
	party leader	music teacher

saw an example of this latter pattern with the shift from "scene of the crime" to "crime scene".

Table 7.6 contains the ten most frequent NN sequences for the two semantic categories in the first and last time period. In the earlier time period, the easiest NN sequences to explain are *slave trade* – slavery officially ended in the United States in 1865 – and *war chief*, a reference to military leaders in wars between US troops and Native Americans that concluded around the turn of the twentieth century.

In the earlier time period, there are thirteen references to government entities in the Institution category and government jobs in the Specialization category, compared with only four in the later time period. We might suppose, based on this, that references to government entities and roles are becoming less common. This is clearly not the case; the US government has greatly expanded its powers (Ford, 1909; Orbach, Callahan, & Lindemenn, 2010), as well as the number of government employees and expenditures per capita (Bryant, 1998). Instead, a look at the NN sequences farther down the list reveals that there is just a much larger proportion of the NN sequences that refer to private entities (often corporations) and employment (*stock market, grocery story, insurance company, law firm, oil company, radio station, gas station, defense attorney*). This cannot be explained by any one historical change in the United States. Rather, it is probably related to a confluence of factors, including rapid technological advances that introduced new sources of employment, the Industrial Revolution and subsequent specialization of labor, and the advent and expansion of the stock market, to mention just a few. In terms of individual lexical items, it seems that the increases in NN frequency are a result of two diachronic changes: (1) many new words entering the language and (2) existing words becoming more frequent, often because they are taking on new meanings. These changes also coincide with new discoveries and inventions, such as fossil fuels, combustible engines, and radio transmission.

NN sequences related to education are more common in the later time period (seven compared with one). These include NN sequences related to school counseling, which did not emerge until the late 1800s (Schimmel, 2008), as well as graduate school (*graduate student, law school*), which did not become common in the United States until the latter half of the nineteenth century (Geiger, 1997).

One of the most frequent Specialization NN sequences in the earlier time period is *bosom friend*. A closer analysis of this term reveals a historical explanation that we have not encountered thus far. According to the Oxford English Dictionary, *bosom friend* refers to "a specially intimate or beloved friend".[26] While one interpretation of the decline (see Figure 7.4) in use of this term could be that Americans do not have close friends anymore, or at least do not write about them as much, an alternative explanation – which seems to be the correct one – is that one or more other terms have replaced *bosom friend* to refer to the same concept. Figures 7.5 and 7.6 display the diachronic trend for *best friend* and *close friend*, respectively. It seems that good friends have not declined; in fact, a look at the per million frequencies suggests the opposite. It is just that we tend to use other pre-modifiers to describe them.

In this section, we have demonstrated how sociohistorical research can be employed to interpret and contextualize quantitative corpus linguistic findings. Two of the NN sequence categories that have experienced the most rapid historical frequency increases were analyzed to identify explanations for these diachronic trends. In addition to a general shift toward using dense noun phrase structures, such as NN sequences, we identified several historical changes that can help explain the linguistic findings. These include changes to legislation (e.g. end of slavery, increase in power of federal government, end of the

---

[26] www.oed.com/view/Entry/21765?redirectedFrom=bosom+friend#eid.

SECTION	ALL	1810	1820	1830	1840	1850	1860	1870	1880	1890	1900	1910	1920	1930	1940	1950	1960	1970	1980	1990	2000
FREQ	169	4	12	12	27	12	16	19	14	8	11	8	7	4	6	1	2	0	1	2	3
WORDS (M)	405	1.2	6.9	13.8	16.0	16.5	17.1	18.6	20.3	20.6	22.1	22.7	25.7	24.6	24.3	24.5	24.0	23.8	25.3	27.9	29.6
PER MIL	0.42	3.39	1.73	0.87	1.68	0.73	0.94	1.02	0.69	0.39	0.50	0.35	0.27	0.16	0.25	0.04	0.08	0.00	0.04	0.07	0.10
SEE ALL YEARS AT ONCE																					

Figure 7.4 Frequency of *bosom friend* per million words by decade (1810–2009) in COHA[27]

---

[27] Corpus data from Davies (2010).

SECTION	ALL	1810	1820	1830	1840	1850	1860	1870	1880	1890	1900	1910	1920	1930	1940	1950	1960	1970	1980	1990	2000
FREQ	2603	7	22	48	30	46	71	62	71	76	104	86	117	81	115	127	129	147	186	370	708
WORDS (M)	405	1.2	6.9	13.8	16.0	16.5	17.1	18.6	20.3	20.6	22.1	22.7	25.7	24.6	24.3	24.5	24.0	23.8	25.3	27.9	29.6
PER MIL	0.42	5.93	3.18	3.48	1.87	2.79	4.16	3.34	3.49	3.69	4.71	3.79	4.56	3.29	4.72	5.17	5.38	6.17	7.35	13.24	23.95
SEE ALL YEARS AT ONCE																					

Figure 7.5 Frequency of *best friend* per million words by decade (1810–2009) in COHA

SECTION	ALL	1810	1820	1830	1840	1850	1860	1870	1880	1890	1900	1910	1920	1930	1940	1950	1960	1970	1980	1990	2000
FREQ	747	0	0	0	3	1	1	2	8	8	20	16	57	55	48	62	80	98	93	85	109
WORDS (M)	405	1.2	6.9	13.8	16.0	16.5	17.1	18.6	20.3	20.6	22.1	22.7	25.7	24.6	24.3	24.5	24.0	23.8	25.3	27.9	29.6
PER MIL	1.84	0.00	0.00	0.00	0.19	0.06	0.06	0.11	0.39	0.44	0.91	0.70	2.22	2.24	1.97	2.53	3.34	4.12	3.67	3.04	3.69
SEE ALL YEARS AT ONCE																					

Figure 7.6 Frequency of *close friend* per million words by decade (1810–2009) in COHA

American Indian Wars), expansion of private corporations and jobs in industry and technology, and increased emphasis on the education system, particularly on higher education. Finally, we discovered that some historical changes correspond to shifts in terminology (e.g. *bosom friend → best friend, close friend*) rather than to historical changes in society and culture.

In this case study, we focused on an investigation of how diachronic changes in NN sequence use can provide insights into cultural, societal, and technological changes in the United States. However, it should be noted that additional analyses would need to be carried out to tease apart the potentially confounding effects of syntactic change in the noun phrase and extralinguistic changes due to shifts in culture, society, and technology.

7.5 Conclusion

In this section, we have argued that quantitative, automated corpus analysis can distract corpus linguists from the goals of describing and interpreting language use, development, variation, and change. We have provided an overview of approaches that corpus linguists can draw on to aid them in their efforts to qualitatively interpret quantitative corpus-based results. We attempted to illustrate some of these approaches through three case studies.

In the case studies, we showed that quantitative findings are not always what they seem. The first case study shows that collocational patterns can rarely be interpreted outside of the linguistic contexts in which they occur. Likewise, in the second case study, we showed that most lexico-grammatical features are multi-functional. As a result, it is not adequate to base functional interpretations on simple rates of occurrence for or correlations among linguistic features. The third case study shows how crucial it is to account for sociohistorical context when interpreting diachronic trends. Patterns of historical change can often be brought to life only with the help of information about and developments in society, politics, medicine, and technology.

Key Considerations:
- Linguistics is done by linguists, not by computers.
- In order to be useful, quantitative corpus linguistic analysis should be coupled with sound qualitative interpretation.
- Researchers can rely on linguistic context, text-external context, and linguistic theory to guide their interpretation of quantitative corpus findings.

8 Wrapping Up

The goal of this Element has been to explore ways for us to improve how we approach linguistic research questions with quantitative corpus data. We began with an analogy with the aim of highlighting why drivers need to know how their vehicles work. Survey research has shown that drivers know much less about the basic mechanics of vehicles than they did in previous generations.[28] One reason for this trend could be that vehicles have become much more mechanically complex in recent decades. As a result, drivers are probably more likely to outsource even basic car maintenance to professionals.

Without deliberate effort, we may see a similar trend in corpus linguistics, with an ever-widening gap between the everyday user and the language contained in a corpus. Our goal is not to suggest that every quantitative corpus linguist needs to become an expert corpus designer, computer programmer, and statistician. But we believe that we all need to be able to "look under the hood" at each stage of the research process and have at least a fundamental understanding of what is going on linguistically. That is why we have written this Element. We hope that we have illustrated some advantages of working toward such an understanding, as well as some of the pitfalls of not doing so.

There are many good reasons for us to keep linguistics at center stage in corpus linguistic research. To this end, we have proposed some ways in which researchers can make more deliberate decisions, always focusing on the end goal of turning corpus-based *data* into meaningful linguistic *information*.

It is not uncommon for the words "data" and "information" to be used interchangeably, as if they meant the same thing. Take, for example, this definition of *data* from an online encyclopedia (emphases added): "**Data** is distinct pieces of **information**, usually formatted in a special way. ... Since the mid-1900s, people have used the word **data** to mean **computer information** that is transmitted or stored" (www.webopedia.com/TERM/D/data.html).

In contrast, scholars in the field of knowledge management have argued that there is an important distinction between "data" and "information". For example (emphases added):

> **Data** are symbols that represent the properties of objects and events. They are to **information** what iron ore is to iron: nothing can be done with **data** until they are processed into **information**. **Information** also consists of symbols that represent the properties of objects and events, but these are symbols that have been processed into a potentially useful message. **Information** is contained in descriptions, answers to questions that begin with such words as *who, where, when,* and *how many* (Ackoff, 2010: 106).

---

[28] www.cheapcarinsurance.net/americas-automotive-iq/

In other words, "**[i]nformation** is born when **data** are interpreted" (Stallings, 1989: 2).

In very general terms, this is the fundamental difference that we have focused on in the present Element. Corpus analysis has been strongly influenced by the "big data" movement. Some corpora are now thousands (and even millions) of times larger than corpora in the twentieth century, and powerful software tools are publicly available that can identify patterns in such corpora. The strength of the big data approach is that we can discover patterns in language data that would never have been detected otherwise. However, the major risk is that such "data" can easily be treated as if it were "information". We have argued here that this is a false equivalence for studies in corpus linguistics. That is, the "data" from quantitative corpus analysis requires linguistic interpretation at every stage in order to qualify as meaningful "information" about language structure and use. In other words, statistical analysis can provide us with data, but that data must be interpreted if it is to be useful for linguistic description.

There is a need for such linguistic interpretation at every step of a corpus analysis. This begins with creating or selecting an appropriate corpus. As discussed in Section 2, researchers will benefit from evaluating the sample of texts in a corpus to determine what discourse domain it represents. Quantitative patterns become linguistically meaningful only when they are interpreted relative to the targeted discourse domain, and only when we have critically evaluated the extent to which our corpus is representative of that domain.

Second, we need to begin with a meaningful linguistic research question, and to design our corpus study so that it can actually answer that question. Corpus analyses will always generate quantitative data. It is thus up to the researcher to ensure that the data actually characterizes the observational units of interest (e.g. texts or word tokens or grammatical feature tokens). Similarly, the researcher must ensure that the data relates to the linguistic characteristics that are important for the research question, that is, the linguistic variables, as shown in Sections 3 and 4.

Corpus analysis software is now capable of producing many different kinds of data extracted from a corpus. In some cases, that data is simply not interpretable in linguistic terms because there is not adequate documentation of how linguistic phenomena are identified in texts or of how measures are calculated. In other cases, it is possible to evaluate the linguistic accuracy of automatic analyses, and possible to interpret quantitative measures in linguistic terms – but doing so often requires considerable work on the part of the researcher, as illustrated in Section 5. Our main argument in this Element is that such work is a necessity. It is very tempting to use a large available corpus, to analyze that corpus with powerful software tools, and to treat the quantitative results as if they were the final product of a principled linguistic inquiry. But this is almost never the case. Rather, the results of such corpus analyses should normally be treated as quantitative data, requiring extensive checking, evaluation, and interpretation before it can be presented as information in the form of language description.

One major challenge in this regard is that corpus-builders and corpus-tool-developers usually refer to their corpora and tools with linguistically meaningful labels; as a result, end-users may be persuaded to simply accept the accuracy of those labels. We, instead, urge end-users to be skeptical of such labels. A corpus might be labeled "academic writing" and actually contain informational blogs. A grammatical tagger might claim to identify nouns and verbs in a corpus, but it will usually mis-identify the part of speech for a particular word of interest. A corpus analysis tool might automatically compute a measure labeled "cohesion" but actually just count the frequency of definite articles or pronouns. Here, as elsewhere, it is the responsibility of the end-user to ensure that they understand the linguistic basis of all corpora and all corpus analysis tools.

Finally, we have discussed in detail in Sections 6 and 7 the two sides of any linguistically meaningful quantitative corpus analysis: the statistical analysis and the qualitative interpretation. We have argued that researchers should make deliberate choices about the statistical technique that best fits their research goals, ideally using minimally sufficient statistical measures. Typically, a statistical analysis will produce many types of quantitative data. A researcher should be able to reconcile the apparent patterns emerging from this data – and, most importantly, the researcher should always interpret the results of statistical analyses through consideration of actual texts. If a statistical analysis indicates that a linguistic feature is more frequent in certain kinds of texts or in certain linguistic contexts, we should be able to observe the linguistic phenomena in the corpus. Detailed consideration of linguistic context will always aid in the linguistic interpretation. In short, we recommend interpretation of quantitative data as linguistic patterns, based on inspection of the linguistic features in texts.

In summary, the primary message of the present Element is twofold: (1) that corpus analyses should always be linguistically interpretable, making them corpus *linguistic* studies, and (2) that it is the responsibility of the end-researcher to ensure that quantitative corpus data is evaluated, appropriately analyzed, and interpreted, transforming the data into linguistically meaningful information.

To facilitate further discussion about the topics addressed in the Element, we have established a blog titled "Linguistics with a Corpus" where we plan to post regularly on pertinent topics related to the themes addressed in this Element. We hope that this blog will be a helpful source of information and education about issues related to research design in corpus linguistics. We also hope that the blog will be a useful discussion forum for researchers to ask questions and engage in dialogue about solutions to their research design challenges.

Appendix
Why It Is Problematic to Apply NHST to Large (Corpus) Samples

The two characteristics of every NHST are the size of the effect and the size of the sample(s).[1] We will here use the formula for an independent samples t test as an example; the formula looks as follows:

$$t = \frac{M_1 - M_2}{SD_p \sqrt{\frac{2}{n}}}$$

In this formula, the numerator contains the difference between the two group means and the denominator contains the pooled standard deviation multiplied by the square root of 2 divided by n. It can be seen from this formula that there are two main ways to increase t (and thus reduce the p-value associated with it): (1) increase the size of the magnitude of the difference between the two means (relative to their pooled standard deviation), and (2) increase the size of n. While it makes sense for statistical formulas to account for n size for the sake of statistical power, there is a reality here that is rarely acknowledged: as n increases, t will also increase, even if the overall effect of a difference or relationship remains the same. Taken to an extreme, this means that, at some point, any effect, no matter how small, will result in a large t value and a small p-value (thus possibly leading a researcher to reject the null hypothesis).

Using and reporting on measures of effect size is therefore imperative in quantitative corpus linguistics if the researcher is to gain insights into the practical significance of research findings. An effect size is a standardized measure of the magnitude of the difference between two groups or the relationship between two variables. One of the major advantages of using measures of effect size is that the result does not normally rely on the size of the sample.[2] A commonly used measure of effect size for comparisons of group means is Cohen's d. The formula for Cohen's d is:

---

[1] While we will here focus on comparisons between two groups, and independent samples t tests, the inverse relationship between n size and p-value exists within all NHST techniques within the frequentist paradigm, including chi-square, correlations, ANOVAs, regressions, and many multivariate techniques.

[2] Cramer's V and phi are measures of effect size for the chi-square statistic, and both divide the chi-square result by n in order to place the measure on a standard scale and account for the fact that the chi-square statistic always increases as n increases.

$$d = \frac{M_1 - M_2}{SD_p}$$

It can be seen that the only difference between this formula and the formula for t already shown is the absence of the $\sqrt{\frac{2}{n}}$ term in the denominator. Although Cohen's d does not allow one to make any claims about statistical significance, it is a powerful tool for accounting for group differences on a continuous standard scale, with no issues related to overpowered (or underpowered) samples.

The influence of n in the t formula (and the corresponding p-value) can be seen in this table, where the descriptive statistics (i.e. M_1, M_2, and SD_p) and the Cohen's d effect size are held constant across different sample sizes. As is shown, the p-value drops steadily as the n size increases. At $n = 75$, it reaches the point where it is significant at the $p < .05$ level, and already at $n = 125$, it is significant at the $p < .01$ level.

n	M_1	M_2	SD_p	Cohens d	t-statistic	p-value
25	5	4	3	0.33	1.18	0.250
50	5	4	3	0.33	1.67	0.102
75	5	4	3	0.33	2.04	0.045
100	5	4	3	0.33	2.36	0.020
125	5	4	3	0.33	2.64	0.009

In short, if you hold an effect size constant and increase the n size, the p-value will decrease until it is well below any pre-established alpha criterion, despite the fact that the effect has not increased and may be insignificant for all practical purposes. Corpus linguistic data can be particularly susceptible to this weakness of NHST because it often comes in extremely large samples.

References

Ackoff, R. L. (2010). *Systems Thinking for Curious Managers*. Chicago: Triarchy Press.

Anthony, L. (2013). A critical look at software tools in corpus linguistics. *Linguistics Research*, 30(2), 141–61.

Anthony, L. & Baker, P. (2015). ProtAnt: A tool for analysing the prototypicality of texts. *International Journal of Corpus Linguistics*, 20(3), 273–92.

Baayen, H. R., Janda, L. A., Nesset, T., Endresen, A., & Makarova, A. (2013). Making choices in Russian: Pros and cons of statistical methods for rival forms. *Russian Linguistics*, 37(3), 253–91.

Baker, P. (2004). Querying keywords: Questions in difference, frequency, and sense in keyword analysis. *Journal of English Linguistics*, 32(4), 346–59.

Baker, P. (2010). Corpus methods in linguistics. In L. Litosseliti, ed. *Research Methods in Linguistics*. New York: Continuum, pp. 95–113.

Biber, D. (1984). A model of textual relations within the written and spoken modes. Unpublished PhD dissertation. Los Angeles: University of Southern California.

Biber, D. (1988). *Variation across Speech and Writing*. Cambridge: Cambridge University Press.

Biber, D. (1993). Representativeness in corpus design. *Literary and Linguistic Computing*, 8(4), 243–57.

Biber, D. (2006). *University Language: A Corpus-Based Study of Spoken and Written Registers*. Amsterdam: John Benjamins.

Biber, D. (2009). A corpus-driven approach to formulaic language in English: Multi-word patterns in speech and writing. International journal of corpus linguistics, 14(3), 275–311.

Biber, D. & Conrad, S. (2019). *Register, Genre, and Style* (2nd ed.). Cambridge: Cambridge University Press.

Biber, D. & Egbert, J. (2018). *Register Variation Online*. Cambridge: Cambridge University Press.

Biber, D., Johansson, S., Leech, G., Conrad, S., & Finegan, E. (1999). *The Longman Grammar of Spoken and Written English*. London: Longman.

Biber, D. & Jones, J. K. (2009). Quantitative methods in corpus linguistics. In A. Lüdeling & M. Kytö, eds. *Corpus Linguistics: An International Handbook*. Berlin: Walter de Gruyter, pp. 1286–1304.

Biber, D., Reppen, R., Schnur, E., & Ghanem, R. (2016). On the (non)utility of Juilland's D to measure lexical dispersion in large corpora. *International Journal of Corpus Linguistics*, 21(4), 439–64.

Biber, D., Staples, S., Gray, B., & Egbert, J. (2020). Investigating grammatical complexity in L2 English writing research: Linguistic description versus predictive measurement. *Journal of English for Academic Purposes*.

Blair, E. & Blair, J. (2015). *Applied Survey Sampling*. London: Sage.

Brezina, V. (2018). *Statistics in Corpus Linguistics: A Practical Guide*. Cambridge: Cambridge University Press.

Bryant, J. (1998). The Great Depression and New Deal. http://teachersinstitute .yale.edu/curriculum/units/1998/4/98.04.04.x.html.

Caldas-Coulthard, C. R. & Moon, R. (2010). "Curvy, hunky, kinky": Using corpora as tools for critical analysis. *Discourse & Society*, 21(2), 99–133.

Carroll, J. B., Davies, P., & Richman, B. (1971). The American Heritage word frequency book. Houghton Mifflin.

Chen, D. & Manning, C. (2014). A fast and accurate dependency parser using neural networks. In Proceedings of the 2014 Conference on Empirical Methods in Natural Language Processing. Association for Computational Linguistics, pp. 740–50.

Clear, J. (1992). Corpus sampling. In G. Leitner, ed., *New Directions in Language Corpora: Methodology, Results, Software Developments*. Berlin: De Gruyter, pp. 21–32.

Cohen, J. (1977). *Statistical Power Analysis for the Behavioral Sciences*. New York: Routledge.

Davies, M. (2010–) *The Corpus of Historical American English (COHA): 400 million words, 1810–2009*. Available online at www.english-corpora.org/coha/.

Egbert, J. (2014). Reader Perceptions of Linguistic Variation in Published Academic Writing. Unpublished PhD dissertation. Flagstaff: Northern Arizona University.

Egbert, J. (2015). Sub-register and discipline variation in published academic writing: Investigating statistical interaction in corpus data. *International Journal of Corpus Linguistics*, 20(1), 1–29.

Egbert, J. (2019). Corpus design and representativeness. In T. Berber Sardinha & M. Veirano Pinto, eds., *Multi-dimensional Analysis: Research Methods and Current Issues*. London: Bloomsbury, pp. 27–42.

Egbert, J. & Baker, P. eds. (2019). *Using Corpus Methods to Triangulate lLnguistic Analysis*. New York: Routledge.

Egbert, J. & Biber, D. (2019). Incorporating text dispersion into keyword analyses. *Corpora*, 14(1), 77–104.

Egbert, J., Burch, B., & Biber, D. (2020). Lexical dispersion and corpus design. *International Journal of Corpus Linguistics*, 25(1), 89–115.

Egbert, J., & Davies, M. (2019). If olive oil Is made of olives, then what's baby oil made of?: The shifting semantics of noun+ noun sequences in American English. In J. Egbert and P. Baker (Eds.), Using corpus methods to triangulate linguistic analysis (pp. 163–184). New York City: Routledge.

Ellis, N. (2019). Usage-based theories of Construction Grammar: Triangulating corpus linguistics and psycholinguistics. In J. Egbert & P. Baker, eds. (2019). *Using Corpus Methods to Triangulate Linguistic Analysis.* New York: Routledge.

Evert, S. (2004). The statistics of word cooccurrences: Word pairs and collocations. Unpublished PhD thesis. Stuttgart: University of Stuttgart.

Evert, S. (2009). Corpora and collocations. In A. Lüdeling & M. Kytö, eds. *Corpus Linguistics: An International Handbook*, Vol. 2. Berlin/New York: Mouton de Gruyter, pp. 1212–48.

Ford, H. J. (1909). The influence of state politics in expanding federal power. *Proceedings of the American Political Science Association*, 5, 53–63.

Gabrielatos, C. (2018). Keyness analysis: Nature, metrics and techniques. In C. Taylor & A. Marchi, eds. *Corpus Approaches to Discourse: A Critical Review.* London/New York: Routledge, pp. 225–58.

Geiger, R. L. (1997). Research, graduate education, and the ecology of American universities: An interpretive history. In L. F. Goodchild & H. S. Weschler, eds. *The History of Higher Education* (2nd ed.). Needham Heights: Simon & Schuster, pp. 273–89.

Graesser, A. C., McNamara, D. S., & Louwerse, M. M. (2003). What do readers need to learn in order to process coherence relations in narrative and expository text? In A. P. Sweet & C. E. Snow, eds. *Rethinking Reading Comprehension.* New York: Guilford Publications, pp. 82–98.

Gries, S. T. (forthcoming). On classification trees and random forests in corpus linguistics: Some words of caution and suggestions for improvement. *Corpus Linguistics and Linguistic Theory.*

Hanks, P. (2012). The corpus revolution in lexicography. *International Journal of Lexicography*, 25(4), 398–436.

Hasselgård, H. (2010). *Adjunct Adverbials in English.* Cambridge: Cambridge University Press.

Hinrichs, L. & Szmrecsanyi, B. (2007). Recent changes in the function and frequency of Standard English genitive constructions: A multivariate analysis of tagged corpora. *English Language & Linguistics*, 11(3), 437–74.

Hinrichs, L., Szmrecsanyi, B., & Bohmann, A. (2015). Which-hunting and the Standard English relative clause. Language, 91(4), 806–836.

Housen, A., De Clercq, B., Kuiken, F., & Vedder, I. (2019). Multiple approaches to complexity in second language research. *Second Language Research*, 35(1), 3–21. Published online (2018). https://doi.org/10.1177/0267658318809765.

Hunston, S. (2002). Corpora in applied linguistics. Cambridge: Cambridge University Press.

Hunston, S. (2007). Semantic prosody revisited. *International Journal of Corpus Linguistics*, 12(2), 249–68.

Hunt, K. W. (1970). Do sentences in the second language grow like those in the first? *TESOL Quarterly*, 4(3), 195–202.

Larsson, T., Callies, M., Hasselgård, H., Laso, N. J., Van Vuuren, S., Verdaguer, I., & Paquot, M. (2020). Adverb placement in EFL academic writing: Going beyond syntactic transfer. International Journal of Corpus Linguistics, 25(2), 155–184.

Larsson, T. & Kaatari, H. (2020). Syntactic complexity across registers: Investigating (in)formality in second-language writing. *Journal of English for Academic Purposes*, 45, 100850.

Larsson, T., Paquot, M., & Plonsky, L. (forthcoming). Inter-rater reliability in learner corpus research: Insights from a collaborative study on adverb placement. *International Journal of Learner Corpus Research*.

Leech, G. (2007). New resources, or just better old ones? The Holy Grail of representativeness. In M. Hundt, N., Nesselhauf, & C. Biewer, eds. *Corpus Linguistics and the Web*. Amsterdam: Brill Rodopi, pp. 133–50.

Leech, G., Hundt, M., Mair, C., & Smith, N. (2009). *Change in Contemporary English: A Grammatical Study*. Cambridge: Cambridge University Press.

Levshina, N. (2015). *How to Do Linguistics with R: Data Exploration and Statistical Analysis*. Amsterdam: John Benjamins.

Levshina, N. (forthcoming). Conditional Inference Trees and Random Forests. In S. Th. Gries & M. Paquot, eds. A Practical Handbook of Corpus Linguistics. New York: Springer.

Lu, X. (2010). Automatic analysis of syntactic complexity in second language writing. *International Journal of Corpus Linguistics*, 15(4), 474–96.

Lu, X. (2017). Automated measurement of syntactic complexity in corpus-based L2 writing research and implications for writing. *Language Testing*, 34(4), 493–511.

McEnery, T., Xiao, R., & Tono, Y. (2006). *Corpus-Based Language Studies: An Advanced Resource Book*. New York: Taylor & Francis.

Nivre, J., Hall, J., Nilsson, J., Chanev, A., Eryigit, G., Kubler, S., Marinov, S., & Marsi, E. (2007). MALTparser: A language-independent system for data-driven dependency parsing. *Natural Language Engineering*, 13(2), 95–135.

Orbach, B., Callahan, K. S., & Lindemenn, L. M. (2010). Arming states' rights: Federalism, private lawmakers, and the battering ram strategy. *Arizona Law Review*, 52, 1161–1206.

Picoral, A., Reppen, R., & Staples, S. (under review). Evaluation of annotation resources for learner data: A comparison of software tools. Special Issue of International Journal of Learner Corpus Research, Natural Language Processing for Learner Corpus Research.

Quirk, R., Greenbaum, S., Leech, G., & Svartvik, J. (1985). *A Comprehensive Grammar of the English Language*. London: Longman.

R Core Team (2020). R: A language and environment for statistical computing. Vienna: R Foundation for Statistical Computing, www.R-project.org/.

Rychlý, P. (2008). A lexicographer-friendly association score. In P. Sojka & A. Horák, eds. *Proceedings of Recent Advances in Slavonic Natural Language Processing, RASLAN*. Brno: Masaryk University, pp. 6–9.

Savický, P. & Hlaváčová, J. (2002). Measures of word commonness. *Journal of Quantitative Linguistics*, 9, 215–31.

Schimmel, C. (2008). School counseling: A brief historical overview. *West Virginia Department of Education*. http://wvde.state.wv.us/counselors/history.html.

Scott, M. 1997. PC analysis of key words – and key words. *System*, 25(2), 233–45.

Sinclair, J. (1991). *Corpus, Concordance, Collocation*. Oxford: Oxford University Press.

Stallings, W. (1989). *Data and Computer Communications* (4th ed.). New York: Macmillan.

Strobl, C., Boulesteix, A.-L., Kneib, T., Augustin, T., & Zeileis, A. (2008). Conditional variable importance for random forests.*BMC Bioinformatics*, 9(307), www.biomedcentral.com/1471–2105/9/307.

Stubbs, M. (1995) Corpus evidence for norms of lexical collocation. In G. Cook & B. Seidlhofer, eds. *Principles and Practice in the Study of Language and Learning*. Oxford: Oxford University Press, pp. 245–256.

Szmrecsanyi, B. & Hinrichs, L. (2008). Probabilistic determinants of genitive variation in spoken and written English: A multivariate comparison across time, space, and genres. In T. Nevalainen, I. Taavitsainen, P. Pahta, & M. Korhonen, eds. *The Dynamics of Linguistic Variation: Corpus Evidence on English Past and Present*. Amsterdam: Benjamins, pp. 291–309.

Xiao, R. & McEnery, T. (2006). Collocation, semantic prosody, and near synonymy: A cross-linguistic perspective. *Applied Linguistics*, 27(1), 103–29.

Cambridge Elements ≡

Corpus Linguistics

Elements in the Series

Multimodal News Analysis across Cultures
Helen Caple, Changpeng Huan and Monika Bednarek

*Doing Linguistics with a Corpus: Methodological Considerations
for the Everyday User*
Jesse Egbert, Tove Larsson and Douglas Biber

A full series listing is available at: www.cambridge.org/corpuslinguistics

Printed in the United States
By Bookmasters